HIGHER

LOVE

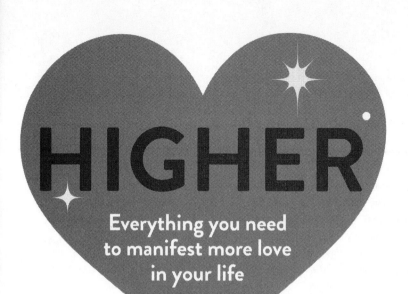

HIGHER

Everything you need
to manifest more love
in your life

LOVE

Jordanna Levin

murdoch books
Sydney | London

Published in 2021 by Murdoch Books,
an imprint of Allen & Unwin

Murdoch Books Australia
83 Alexander Street, Crows Nest NSW 2065
Phone: +61 (0)2 8425 0100
murdochbooks.com.au
info@murdochbooks.com.au

Murdoch Books UK
Ormond House, 26–27 Boswell Street, London WC1N 3JZ
Phone: +44 (0) 20 8785 5995
murdochbooks.co.uk
info@murdochbooks.co.uk

A catalogue record for this
book is available from the
National Library of Australia

A catalogue record for this book is available from the British Library
ISBN 978 1 76052 554 5 Australia
ISBN 978 1 91163 278 8 UK

Cover design by Alissa Dinallo
Cover photography by Bayleigh Vedelago
Text design by Alissa Dinallo and Susanne Geppert
Typeset by Susanne Geppert
Printed and bound in Australia by Griffin Press

10 9 8 7 6 5 4 3 2 1

This book is dedicated to Leokadia,
a strong woman in the making.

CONTENTS

I begin this book with a tender heart *1*

I begin this book with a tender heart

In the past, I may have called it broken, but the truth is it's just a little bruised. I spent years avoiding love, avoiding dating, avoiding getting too close to someone in case I got hurt. We all do this to some degree. It comes from past rejections, past disappointments, past pain, past love that we've lost, and before you know it you've built a barricade of walls around not just your heart but your entire vibrational field – too scared to even let a stranger's smile penetrate it.

But, having just experienced a surprisingly epic love story and then having it ripped out from under me (more on that later), I can say that my heart is still beating. Even though I sit here with a heavy heart that is experiencing loss and lack and remnants of emptiness, it's still whole; there are no cracks, no breaks, just lessons and imprinted memories. If I had to sum up what I'm feeling in one word, it's a deep sense of *longing*. A longing for what was, a longing for lost future plans and a serious longing for something that just felt really bloody good.

I know that starting a book about finding love – and not just any love, but a 'higher love' – by recounting a recent relationship ending might seem less than aspirational, but the reason I begin by exposing my tender heart is that I want you to know that love is not something to be feared. Sure, love can be scary, disappointing, confronting, nerve-racking, exposing, exhausting and, at times, frustrating as all hell, but it can also be a prologue to your next chapter.

Do you just want to skip to the bit where you're creating a banging life with your soulmate? Me too! In fact, I wrote an entire book about manifestation called *Make It Happen*, and the chapter on manifesting love is my favourite one of all. But here's the thing: it's a very rare occasion that even an epically manifested love just waltzes into your life, sweeps you off your feet and starts the dream life you envisage from day dot. First, you have to date them, and yeah, let's not sugar-coat it, it's a jungle out there!

This book isn't just going to guide you through the jungle, it's also going to ensure you can hold yourself in that jungle, become the high priestess of that jungle and choose which jungle monkeys (or majestic lions) you want to create a life with.

Often, when we look back on our history with love and even towards our hope for love in the future, it's easy to start thinking, *How did this happen?* or *Why am I single?* While everyone's circumstance is so individual, I can guarantee that we each have a story we've been enacting. Personally, I lost my direction with love because, from a very young age, it felt very much out of my control. Very 'he loves me, he loves me not'. And if he didn't love me, then I was void of love. This type of feeling isn't limited to romantic love, it can also limit how we experience love from our parents, our siblings, our teachers, our peers and even our childhood pets. We decipher our own meaning of love based on how it is shown to us. We'll explore this deeper in a later chapter, but for now, let's just sit with the actuality of it. Many of us base our experience of love on everything that is *outside* of ourselves and, consequently, out of our control.

I recall feeling helpless when it came to who I fell in love with in my twenties. I found myself always falling for the men who chose me. Often, I wouldn't really feel attracted to them at all, and in some cases, I'd even find them somewhat irritating. But, if they showed enough persistence, and mixed that with promises and compliments, I would soon find myself falling for them – it was almost as if I had no choice in the matter. And I don't know about you, but once I fall, I fall hard. It starts with a gentle push and then, before I know it, I'm plummeting far too quickly to be saved. And then that love roller-coaster swings into full gear.

This happened to me again quite recently. To all intents and purposes, I had entered into a fling with zero intention of 'falling'. The relationship was going to be fun, light and superficial at best – nothing serious. But then, without much warning, I tripped over my own good intentions and fell 'head over heels' for Jack (you'll meet this fella a bit later).

It's a strange expression, 'to be head over heels' – I mean, your head is always over your heels, unless you're in a yoga inversion or handstand, but again, this feeling of *tripping*, *falling*, landing all *topsy-turvy* became the indication that I had, indeed, against my better judgement, begun a deep descent into love, or something like it.

In my case, this falling has never ended well; I generally end up feeling love for someone who is unable to love me back. Perhaps this is why we talk about falling in the context of love. It plays into the tragedy and helplessness of it all. You see, it's so powerless to 'fall' in love. That feeling that the solid ground you once knew has seemingly disappeared from under your feet and, whether you want to or not, you're headed into the depths of 'love'.

But what if we changed the idea of 'falling in love' to 'rising in love'? What if, instead of descending into a powerless pit of helplessness, we strove to ascend to a higher love (see what I did there)? Now that's a romantic idea I can get behind.

To create a higher love – a nourishing, strong, vibrant relationship – it's so important that you walk into it as a nourished, strong, vibrant and whole being. (Note that no one is saying 'perfect'.) You're not walking in as a damsel in distress looking for a knight in shining armour.

You are not a riddle looking for a problem-solver, not a lonely soul looking for someone to binge Netflix with, but a soul with a strong sense of self looking to form a rocking relationship. I am THAT excited to show you how to create that, tender heart and all.

I am also excited to show you that finding love isn't a purely external pursuit. The love we have for ourselves is equally important, if not more. In fact, it's kind of the key to everything. That's why, in addition to exploring the world of love and dating, we'll also be figuring out who you are, what lights you up and how you can create a life you love so you can ride the waves of dating with your sense of self intact.

Before we get started, I should say something straight off: I am a white heterosexual woman who dates men, and most of this book is written from my personal experience. That said, I do strongly believe that the messages in this book are universal. If the gender or sexuality references here don't fit your experience of love, I hope that you can still extract some truth from them and apply them in a way that honours you. Love is love, after all.

ONE MORE THING...

The names and identifying details in the stories that follow have been changed to protect the privacy of these individuals – so please don't go trying to play detective.

PART ONE

YOUR PERSONAL VIBRATION

The quest for love is not an adventure I had intended to be on for almost two decades. When I was 16, and fittingly sweet, I envisaged putting a ring on it by age 23, a baby in it by age 26 and weaving a love story through it to last a lifetime. Instead, I found myself strapped into a drama-fuelled love roller-coaster at 17 and struggling to find the let-me-off-this-thing eject button.

I've been lucky to have experienced young love, big love, messy love and convenient love. I've been through bouts where I've dated frequently or infrequently, and I've also been through dry spells that have lasted three years. I've wined and dined with male versions of myself, my parents and been-there-done-that ex-lovers. I've been swept up by romance, side-swiped by swagger and sorely disappointed when a relationship doesn't meet its potential.

Although dating can be so fun, it can also be fraught and, in too many cases, fatally flawed. We become so consumed with impressing, dazzling and being so incredibly sparkly to distract our potential suitor from our many, many flaws – and all the while they're doing the same.

Dating, if we're not doing it consciously – with an eye on our values and what we truly desire – can be something we throw ourselves into with little clarity about the depth, surrounding waters and our ability to stay afloat. And then, before we know it, we're in the middle of the sea with nothing but a self-inflated life vest, a whistle and none of the many fish in said sea that everyone assured you were swimming just below the surface.

What if I were to tell you dating doesn't have to be like this? That there is a way to do it differently – a way that has nothing to do with playing games or remembering one-liners, and absolutely zero to do with the length of your lashes or how fiercely you bat them.

What if the only thing needed for dating with more success was you; but not the insecure, dying-for-validation needy version of you, but rather the 'I am empowered, standing in my truth, know my values and am in full alignment' version of you?

It all comes down to strengthening your personal vibration. You know what a strong vibration attracts? Everything that is in your highest interest, including the love you're longing to create, that you deserve and that you are oh so worthy of.

Consider this your all-access pass to a higher love.

- Chapter 1 -

Your personal vibration and why it's so important

Before you even contemplate dipping your toe in the dating pool (there's no actual pool, FYI, so no risk of actual drowning), it's imperative that you are vibrating at your strongest, most authentic frequency. If you've automatically envisaged yourself pulsating down the street like a life-sized vibrator, let me stop you right there! Your vibration is your energetic make-up. It's what creates your personal energy, and, in terms of manifestation, it's what attracts things into your magnetic field. Dating aside, a healthy, vibrant and radiant personal vibration has the ability to attract incredible, advantageous and seemingly miraculous opportunities, experiences, and yes, people, into your orbit.

I feel you're eager to move forward, love magnet and all that, but before we do, let me catch you up on the concept of manifestation, because it's an important piece of the dating puzzle that I'm going to help you master.

Manifestation, for the uninitiated, is basically the process through which you take ownership of your future and the life that you want to create for yourself. Although this is not a book about manifestation (I already wrote that one), manifestion will come up a lot, because if creating a healthy, nourishing and love-fuelled relationship is your end goal, then YOU are the one who is going to have to *Make It Happen* (title of said manifestation book, if you're in the market. No pressure).

The manifestation formula that I teach, aka the Manifestation Equation, is based on four universal laws: the Law of Attraction, the Law of Vibration, the Law of Action and the Law of Rhythms, and you'll notice that these come up throughout this book in no particular order.

The Manifestation Equation looks like this:
Thoughts + Feelings + Actions + Faith = Manifestation

Only when all four parts of the equation are working together in unison is successful manifestation possible. In this chapter we're going to pay particular attention to our feelings because this is what forms our frequency (more on this in a minute). But having a broad overview of the equation and its role in creating the things in your life you desire – a hot date/life partner/summer fling/soulmate – will help you understand why your personal vibration is so important.

Thoughts (Law of Attraction)
Thoughts are based on the Law of Attraction, the most recognised of the universal laws, which states that **like attracts like.** Basically, positive thoughts create a positive outcome and negative thoughts create a negative outcome, and while this is

so very, very true, thoughts alone are not enough to make a significant impact on our manifestations (mainly because 85 per cent of our thoughts aren't even flippin' true). Think of all the untruths you tell yourself about relationships: *I'll never meet someone. All the good ones are taken. No one will ever love me.* Or the classic, *I'm going to die alone.* We seem to get more and more dramatic the more we allow ourselves to get carried away by our thoughts. And while these thoughts alone are not enough to ensure our destiny as a hermit, they are enough to put blockades and obstacles in our path. To give our thoughts a little juice, we need to be able to place feelings behind them.

Feelings (*Law of Vibration*)

Feelings are based on the Law of Vibration, a universal law that states that **everything in the universe vibrates on its own frequency, and things with a similar frequency are drawn together.** We are going to be working with this particular law throughout the first two parts of this book. Our feelings are what primarily impact our vibrational frequency, and by concentrating on how we want to feel within ourselves and, ultimately, within a new relationship, we can cultivate the vibrations needed to attract that very thing into our lives. In the context of dating, we're talking about that feeling when you really 'vibe' with someone. You know the one: sparks fly, you feel at ease – sexy even. The conversation flows, banter is strong and yeah, most of the time it's unexplainable. This is commonly referred to as chemistry – I like to call it the Law of Vibration in action. But, before we start focusing on the vibrations of others, it is beyond important that we fine-tune our own.

Actions (Law of Action)

The most practical of the universal laws is the Law of Action, which states that **you must do the things and perform the actions necessary to achieve what you are setting out to do.** Want to meet someone to start a beautiful, soulful and passionate relationship with? Well, what are you gonna do about it? Part Three of this book will put you to work, so if you're looking to meet someone, then I'm going to ask you to actually go out and physically date people. (I know, revolutionary!) You'll go beyond writing down a list of traits you're looking for in a partner or creating a vision board of your dream engagement; you'll do more than simply repeat affirmations of love and high vibrations. You'll actually go out into the world and date people, only differently from how you may have done so in the past.

Faith (Law of Rhythm)

When it comes to dating and relationships, faith is a huge component. Faith in yourself, faith in the other person and faith that everything is happening exactly how it should – no amount of pushing, pleading, needing or smothering is going to speed the process up. When it comes to love, relationships and the making of the babies, women, especially, place very strict timelines on themselves. And sure, I get it, biological clocks and all that, but at some point, you're going to need to trust in the timing of your life. It can be a tough pill to swallow for some, but once you do, energetically, you're actually creating a clear and unadulterated path so love can waltz on in.

Faith is one of the hardest things to teach, but for now, all I ask is that you put your faith in me and in the Law of

Rhythm, which states that **all energy in the universe is like a pendulum. It ebbs and flows, waxes and wanes, rises and falls, grows and decays.** As we progress through this book, the Law of Rhythm will start to make more sense, especially in the context of your relationships.

If you came here looking for some serious love advice and you're feeling like perhaps you picked up the wrong book because universal laws = 'woo-woo', I urge you to stick around. We're not going to be casting spells (though if you want to, I won't stop you), we're not going to create a checklist of your non-negotiables when it comes to a future lover and then cross our fingers and hope for the best (not only does that not work, but it also takes away all of your power), and we are absolutely not going to stick affirmations to the mirror that tell you to keep thinking positively, because, although lovely and encouraging, it's just not enough. Sorry.

But before we even contemplate attracting a tall drink of water (I know, you're thirsty), or think about meeting your next lover – your other half, numero uno, your 'plus one'–, it's imperative that we focus on *you* and getting you in tip-top shape. I'm not talking about your booty or your biceps, I'm talking about your vibrational field. Because if you want to attract your perfect match (or at the very least an eligible date) it's important that you know yourself inside and out. You have to be super clear on who you are, what you value, what lights you up, what gives you strength and what drains you, what allows you to be vulnerable, what makes you feel empowered and what brings you fucking joy.

So if we take the teachings of the Law of Vibration and assume that in order to attract what we want into our lives we need to be vibrating on the frequency of the things we're longing to manifest, then it's fair to assume that knowing how to change your vibrational frequency is pretty important, right? Damn straight it is, but here's the thing: while many manifestation and dating texts will tell you to work out what type of partner you want to attract, write down their list of traits and then vibrate on *their* frequency, I'm saying, hang on a goddamn minute! What if you just concentrated on vibrating at *your* most authentic, radiant, strong and powerful frequency, and everything that matches *your* frequency is instantly drawn to *you*.

Sounds much more achievable and sensible, right? To concentrate on making yourself whole and fulfilled rather than trying to find someone to perfectly fill all your empty spaces and gaps and then hope that they stay there forever so you don't come unplugged again. That's why my aim with Part One of this book is to help you get super clear on what makes you 'whole'. We'll identify the frequency of your personal vibration, the ins and outs of what affects it, and explore how you can maintain it when meeting new potential partners so that you're not compromising who you are to suit the person you happen to be dating. #guilty

The self-worth clause you may have missed in the fine print

So, here's a little tidbit that not many people are talking about but everybody should be, because it's LIFE-CHANGING: your level of self-worth and your ability to become a magnetic forcefield that can bring in and attract anything you damn well want are directly correlated! Yep, you're going to find it really hard to manifest in the areas of your life where your self-worth is lacking or you don't feel deserving. In the areas of your life where you feel worthy and deserving, you're going to be a master attractor. And although this applies to anything you're trying to call in, it couldn't be truer when it comes to love and relationships. When I say this to women, more often than not they recite a long list of their friends who are in wonderful relationships but who still have very low levels of self-worth. To which I reply, 'They're probably not in really wonderful relationships, you just think they are. And also, not really my point.'

My main objective here is to help you find that higher love we talked about, and to do that, we've got to get you dating. Yes, dating so *you* can meet 'the one' (or multiple ones – there are multiple, you know). But mostly I just want to get you out there meeting people, forming strong, meaningful connections and discovering more about yourself and what you value. I want to give you the confidence to know that even if you have to kiss a bazillion and one frogs before you find your prince (or tradie, or suit, or digital nomad), you'll come out whole, unbroken and full of hard-learned lessons and new wisdom.

Dating is a vetting process. An opportunity for you to test your own personal vibration out in the real world. But the current reality is that many of us head into the dating scene not really sure of who we are, never mind who or what we want. And if we suffer a few bruises and battle wounds (not actual bruises and wounds – those are *never* okay), we label ourselves 'broken', delete the app and then convince ourselves of the perks of being single. And while there are so many perks to being single, I have a feeling that if you've picked up this book, then staying single is not your end goal.

I spent most of my twenties and early thirties convincing myself that I was going to meet the love of my life in a chance encounter. I didn't need to go out to bars or be on an app, or even be actively dating in any way – he would just find me. And while that is absolutely possible, it's not the most likely scenario (I know, rom-coms have taught you otherwise), and it just makes you a very passive bystander in your own love life. I spent three whole years not going out on a single date. Not one. And when I look back and think about why, I can see that there were a few things going on.

I was fucking terrified. I'd had a messy on-again, off-again saga of a love affair followed by a couple of disappointing half-assed relationships, and honestly, I was terrified of getting my heart broken again.

My self-esteem was non-existent. I didn't feel good about myself inside or out. I hadn't healed or dealt with any of the 'stuff' that had come up in that messy relationship. The truth was, I felt a bit shit about myself, and that shit was packed up in a sweet leather vintage suitcase and carted around to every subsequent relationship I had.

I had no idea who I was. I kind of coasted through life defining myself by the work I did, the suburb I lived in and the friendships I had. But, if you asked me who I was, what lit me up, what my values were and how I felt about this or that, I probably wouldn't have been able to tell you. In a way, it felt safer not knowing who I was and, if I'm going to be super honest, I – like many women – would morph into whatever the next relationship needed me to be in order for it to succeed. But that success was short lived because I was an IMPOSTER.

I had no idea what I wanted. I mean, don't get me wrong, of course I had written a list of traits for my ideal man (several, in fact); are you even a single gal in your twenties if you haven't? But, aside from certain physical attributes and a few key personality traits like being funny and kind, I really wasn't clear on what kind of love I was searching for. I also didn't think I was worthy of receiving a 'dream man', so the list was pretty much just a bunch of words on a scrappy piece of paper.

Although relationship breakdowns are a major contributor to the lowering of one's self-worth, let's not kid ourselves that being single doesn't start to grind on even the highest self-esteem. Trust me, I get it! As an individual who has done a lot of work on raising her self-worth (because, master manifestor) there are still times I look in the mirror and scream, 'HOW AM I 35 AND

STILL SINGLE?' (And, sometimes, 'Who is the fairest of them all?' Just for shits and giggles.)

Am I getting it wrong? What secrets do I not know? Is it my thighs? Am I too intimidating? Too funny? It's because I'm too hilarious, isn't it? One time, after I kept attracting men who said they loved what a go-getter I was until they absolutely did not and found it intimidating AF, I actually said to a girlfriend, 'I think it's time I dull my sparkle.' So, please, let me interject before anyone even contemplates dimming their sparkle. Sometimes you're not necessarily doing anything wrong; sometimes it's all about timing, and perhaps the timing is all about reading this book, implementing some simple tweaks to your personal vibration and getting super clear on what kind of love you want to attract. Your self-worth might need a little work, too, but that's what I'm here for.

Working on improving your self-worth can feel like a chore, but the truth is it's the most beneficial thing you can do for the future you. Like I said before, a high level of self-worth enables you to manifest with ease and success every time. Sure, it's a constant work in progress, but not only will it ensure a better dating experience, it will also guarantee that you come out the other side (relationship or no relationship) as a whole human.

You complete me (and other rubbish things you've heard people say)

It's so freaking romantic to talk about our other halves, missing puzzle pieces and being completed by another, but if you're swanning around town as only half a human with big gaping soul holes on a mission for someone to patch you up, fix you and solve all your problems, well, I'm sorry, but that has to be the *least* attractive, most unromantic thing ever. Harsh, but accurate, no?

In any interaction, romantic or otherwise, it's so important that you walk in as a whole person with a clear set of energetic boundaries. I want you to quit thinking about finding someone to make you feel whole and instead search for someone who complements and adds to the whole version of you. Because don't you want that for your partner, too? You want them to have their shit together, their ducks in a row (insert any metaphor for having their 'stuff' sorted here), so that when you do connect, you can each act as an adornment to the other – the cherry on top or the lashings of chocolate sprinkles if you will. You're not looking to 'fix' each other, fill each other's gaps or patch up each other's wounds – this isn't a DIY renovation show, people! Because if, god forbid, that reno of a relationship ends, you'll be left patching up a bunch of jagged holes, unplugged gaps and, most likely, a bigger mess than you started with. Can you spell disaster?

I've thought a lot about this notion of completeness in the context of dating and what it actually means because I'm not sure if anyone is ever truly complete. As someone who is forever curious, always shifting and transforming, growing and expanding, I don't feel that I'm ever going to reach the point of feeling absolute completeness. It seems a bit final, don't you think? You can, however, in each and every moment, ask yourself, *Am I fulfilling all of my own needs? Is there a part of me that is waiting for someone else to take care of x, y or z? Could*

I potentially look after x, y or z myself? This is not to encourage you to be so independent that you don't have room for anyone to come in and share your life (trust me, I've been there), but rather to encourage you to ask yourself if you're seeking someone who will do the work for you so that you don't have to.

So, right here, right now, let's abolish this whole 'you complete me' bullshit, and even the 'you must complete yourself first' hogwash. Instead, choose to focus on your personal vibration. Because here's the thing about finding completeness in yourself (feel free to take notes): you don't really know how 'complete' you are until you're thrust into a partnership and you start to get poked and prodded – hopefully lovingly – by another person's vibration, with all of their wounds and baggage and flaws. This is why your personal vibration is so important. It allows you to tap in to how aligned you are with your own authenticity in each and every moment. It's also why you need to wrap up past relationship stuff, i.e. find closure (we'll explore this more in chapter 7). Once you have closure, the only other vibration you need be concerned with is that of the person you're dating – not every other person you've dated/slept with/had a crush on in the past (lord knows we're all a little guilty of that!).

What is your personal vibration?

Fine-tuning your vibration might sound saucy, but honestly, of all the concepts I've used to explain manifestation, especially in the context of dating, nothing compares to the power of fine-tuning, honing and strengthening your own personal vibration. If you recall the Law of Vibration, which states that things with a similar frequency are drawn together, working on your own vibration is going to attract everything that is in perfect alignment with you (whether you're aware of it or not). Pretty cool, huh?

Before we create a bangin' (i.e. amazing) personal vibration, it's important to understand exactly what that means. The word 'authenticity' gets thrown around a lot. 'Be your most authentic self,' they say. But when it comes to the crunch, how do we identify our own authenticity, and how can we be sure we're honouring it? There is no prescription for authenticity. It's defined as being real and true. And, at its essence, this is correct. However, this deeply personal feeling of alignment can be easily shifted and influenced by your environment, experiences and the people around you. If you're not in touch with your own authenticity, you'll have zero awareness when it's being compromised.

I prefer to call your authenticity your personal vibration so we can identify what strengthens that vibration and what weakens it – that is, what pulls you into perfect alignment and what pulls you out of it. Let's begin by identifying when you feel most authentic.

In order to properly focus on authenticity, let's first shift our attention to what makes us *feel* most in alignment and allows us to strengthen our vibrational frequency. Grab your journal, it's time for our first exercise ...

IDENTIFYING YOUR PERSONAL VIBRATION

Find a really comfortable spot; the setting isn't too important, only that you feel comfortable and at ease. Close your eyes, centre yourself by taking three deep breaths, and then begin to recall the times in your life when you felt most true to you. Think about times that you feel comfortable and when you are truly able to shine. For me, it's when I'm around certain people and environments. I also tend to feel this way when I'm presenting in front of large groups of people (I recognise that this is unusual); I feel confident, intelligent, funny and witty. Words flow easily, I feel relaxed in my body, I feel incredibly expansive and a real sense of safety sweeps over me.

When does that happen for you? Now imagine yourself fully submerged in that situation. Ask yourself the following questions:

- ♥ *How do I feel in my body?*
- ♥ *Which emotions come easily to me when I feel like the best version of myself?*
- ♥ *What is my posture like?*
- ♥ *How do I communicate?*

This is you at your most authentic, when your personal vibration is strong and firing on all cylinders. Now that you have a sense of when your vibration is strong, let's explore what weakens it. I find that certain people and certain environments weaken my vibration, and I know to avoid them or, if that's not possible, at the very least protect my energy when I'm around them. When I feel uncomfortable (and not just in an out-of-my-comfort-zone kinda way), my posture is closed off, I stumble on my words – or worse, I have nothing to say. My comic timing is a flop, I feel restricted in my body, my energy feels drained and I start to vibrate in a fear state. A weakened vibration may manifest in different ways for you, and it's also really important to recognise that a weakened vibration is not the same as being scared to try something new or being in an unfamiliar environment. There is a subtle difference, and the more familiar you get with how it feels to have a strengthened personal vibration, the more you'll recognise what weakens it. Think about times your vibration has felt compromised and ask yourself:

- ❤ *How do I feel in my body?*
- ❤ *What emotions do I feel?*
- ❤ *What happens to my posture?*
- ❤ *How is my communication affected?*

Now take a piece of paper and draw a line down the centre of the page. On one side of the page write **Strengthens**. On the other side write **Weakens**. You might not have all the answers straight away so, over the next few days, start to record when your vibration feels stronger – in other words, when you feel like the truest and best version of yourself – and when your vibration feels weakened or compromised.

Slowly but surely, you will start to notice which simple and avoidable things, people, environments and experiences weaken your vibrational field. And then you'll be able to make some informed choices.

New phone, who dis?
Identifying your own authenticity

In the next chapter, we're going to dive deeper into identifying, developing and strengthening your personal vibration. Before we do, I must reiterate why this work is so important. So grab your journal again, because I'm about to share some profound wisdom with you. (Suspense builds, author instantly regrets building anticipation, but is confident you'll benefit from the next statement.) Self-awareness is one of four great super-powers needed to live a heart-driven and purpose filled life. The others are intuition, compassion and mutability. But self-awareness allows us to see ourselves in our entirety and be tuned in to the changes taking place within us, so we can be aware of when our values, energy and personal vibration are being compromised unnecessarily. This is so freaking important when it comes to dating.

Having a strong and clear sense of who you are and your own personal vibration before you enter the dating (not actual) pool means you'll be able to treat rejection (eeek), disappoint-ment (awww) or heartbreak (oooh) as experiences rather than reflections of who you are as a person.

- Chapter 2 -

Locating, developing and strengthening your personal vibration

My natural state is not passive aggressive, and I'm not impatient or an icy bitch. Truly! But having just come out of a beautiful, easy, kismet-style relationship in which I was kind, patient, calm and ... look, I'm just gonna come out and say it, a bloody catch, I found myself in the next experience feeling very unlike myself.

The 'myself' I'm referring to is my true self – my best self. The self I like. The self I strive to be. The self that feels effort-less, natural, advantageous and sparkly. And although someone else is not responsible for how you feel, react or express your-self, when it comes to relationships, it is profoundly eye-opening to observe how easily you can be your most natural self and when you can't.

Kurt was a sexy, accomplished, emotionally available and intelligent man. We had a similar sense of humour (well, he laughed at my jokes), and he was looking to settle down and start a family (attractive to 35-year-old me). He was honest, spoke openly about his feelings, loved to make future plans, and complimented me lots (big tick for a Gemini gal).

On paper, it should have worked. We got along, we had enough in common, and also plenty not in common, which is always a bonus in my book. But, for some reason, I just didn't like myself when I was around him. I had a short fuse, I never felt comfortable enough to drop my guard completely, and I struggled to contribute to conversation. Me! Miss Chatterbox. And even though he was gorgeous, sexy (did I mention that already?) and pretty goddamn perfect, he threw off my personal vibration big time.

You might have a similar sense with certain friends or work colleagues. It's not their fault. Or yours. It's an energetic thing. It has little to do with similar interests or backgrounds or whether you both enjoy Quentin Tarantino films, and everything to do with the way you vibrate when you're around them. This is a good indicator of your personal vibration. So when it's firing and going from strength to strength, does that mean you've found your peeps or, in the context of dating, a perfect match? Hmm, not necessarily ...

Jack was not what we ladies would call a classic 'catch'. He didn't tick many of the boxes I *thought* would make up my perfect man. He had just come out of an eight-year relationship, had moved back in with his dad and had several different jobs (none of which he was overly passionate about). He enjoyed a tipple most nights, and, honestly, as I'm writing this I'm thinking, *How the HELL did this work?*

But he was also wonderfully kind, funny (like, so funny), incredibly intelligent, beyond quirky, and challenged me in all the right ways. We had aligned values and visions, our comic timing was on point and I was eternally fascinated by the way he saw the world. When I was around Jack, I never felt more like myself. Jack was the guy I mentioned earlier who made me feel kind, patient, cool, calm and collected. I actually didn't realise that was my natural state until I met him. He highlighted a side of me that I wanted to get to know better. My vibration felt strengthened around him, and I'd be bold enough to say that I strengthened his vibration, too. And consequently, we had a pretty sweet relationship. Does this mean Jack was the guy for me? Evidently no (we'll get to the logistics of that later)! But he highlighted this beautiful contrast that became so apparent when I was with Kurt, and I was able to identify the difference between the true me – who I identified with and wanted to continue to be – and the agitated, bitchy me who was honestly a pain in the ass.

I must make it very clear that the way I felt about myself with Jack and the way I felt with Kurt had nothing to do with them and everything to do with me. My alignment and my vibrations were strengthened and weakened by my choices. But it was only because I had such an acute sense of my own personal vibration that I was able to decipher this.

Identifying your personal vibration

Okay, so now we know the importance of having a finely tuned personal vibration, but if you're struggling to identify what yours is, then there is no way you're going to be able to strengthen it.

Identifying your personal vibration starts with an acute sense of self-awareness. Unless you know full well when your vibration is compromised, how will you know to bring it back into alignment?

My vibration is constantly compromised. Yep. The person teaching you how to strengthen your vibration often finds herself in situations that weaken her own. But when you can identify a weakening of your personal vibration, you can whip it back quick smart. Never is this skill more useful than when dating.

So what makes up a personal vibration? Well, I believe it's a host of things, and the more familiar you get with these contributing factors, the more you can add to them or take away. An important thing to note is that your personal vibration will shift as you do. The frequency might remain the same (and get stronger or weaker in different moments), but what makes up that frequency can, and most likely will, change.

What do you value?

What do you believe in? I'm not talking about ghosts or aliens or the possibility of Elvis still roaming this earth, but rather, what are the fundamental beliefs that make up your personal core values? Unsurprisingly, these values are an intrinsic part of your personal vibration, but the truth is that many of us aren't that clear on what our values are; I know I wasn't.

More often than not, what I thought were *my* values were actually dictated by the values of the people around me – I mean, who even knows if their values are theirs or influenced by the people around them? See the importance of clarity?

I only figured out what my values were a couple of years ago. I may have pondered them in moments when perhaps they were compromised, but I'd never sat down and actively thought about what I truly valued in life or identified what my values were around family, money, relationships, work, etc.

Why are our values so valuable?

Think of your values as the core of your authenticity. They are the stone pillars that allow you to stand confidently in your truth. When they are compromised, the stability of your core is rocked and your tank is all but emptied. This throws off your alignment and is a really obvious indicator of a weakened personal vibration, and this is of particular importance when you're in a relationship with someone. You can have different hobbies, passions and opposing opinions on politics, food and whether Antarctica is a cute or horrific baby name, but if your values (aka a huge part of your personal vibration) aren't aligned, soon enough you're both going to feel the impact of having the core of your being challenged. But if aligned interests, objectives and visions doth not maketh an aligned value, then what does? Good question! We'll talk about aligned values when it comes to relationships, but Part One of this book is all about dating *yourself* and getting to know you better. Believe it or not, your values are at the heart of that, so let's begin by identifying what your core values are.

When I first sat down to list my core values (because lists make things real, right?), the first thing I wanted to do was Google 'common values' or 'what are good values to have?'. Please don't do this. Adopting your values from a list that someone else has compiled is not the way to work out what *you* value. It should be a process of uncovering and discovering. When we work from a list of predetermined values, we start weighing up the importance of one over another.

But I get it, compiling this list can be harder than you think. When I first truly contemplated said values list, I had a mini-meltdown because I'm dramatic like that. Did I even have values? Are x, y and z important to me, or did I just think they should be? How did I get through the first 30 years of my life void of values? But then I broke it down and figured out a really simple and easy way to get to the heart of what matters most. Shall we do it together?

Exercise 2

UNCOVERING YOUR PERSONAL VALUES

Another way of looking at values is to define what means the most to you. What feels important and necessary for you to live a fulfilled life (*feels* being the operative word)? Knowing (or thinking) a value is one thing but when you're in alignment with that value, how does it feel?

Look back on your life and identify when you felt really bloody good. Try to think of scenarios that span different areas of your life, such as relationships, career or finances. When you've identified one of those scenarios, really feel into that moment and answer the following questions.

- ❤ What were you doing?
- ❤ Who was there? Did they contribute to how you felt?
- ❤ What specific feelings did you have in those moments? Happiness, freedom, creativity, abundance, stability, safety and so on? Get curious and keep digging until you uncover every feeling that was present in that scenario.
- ❤ Are there feelings that you long to experience in your life and that you feel are important to you but perhaps you haven't had yet? Or, have you felt the opposite of those feelings and found that they made you feel like shit, which in turn made you realise why it's so goddamn important to experience the feeling you desire?

I think what confused me when I first sat down to write down my values is that I thought they needed to be complete statements that I held myself accountable to. But actually, your core values are *feelings* that you value in your life. Our feelings greatly impact our vibration, so it makes sense that when we're aligned with the ones that feel good we are strengthening our vibration, and when we find ourselves in situations that don't allow us to access those feelings, that might be an indication that our personal vibration is being weakened – as in my relationship with Kurt.

Can you list the feelings that you value as core parts of your vibration? These are feelings that you want to experience through the choices you make throughout your life. Later, when we start talking about aligning our values with those of another person, you will be able to see if any of these core values are worth compromising on; most of the time you will find they are definitely not.

What brings you joy?

Was joy one of your values? It's okay if it wasn't, but I'm about to make a good case for including it. We've all heard tidier-up extraordinaire Marie Kondo talk about how important it is to tap in to joy, and how you can determine whether a household item should stay or go by holding it and asking the question: Does this spark joy? Well, I'm about to encourage you to Marie Kondo your life, because she's onto something with this joy thing.

Let's start by recognising the difference between happiness and joy. Happiness, albeit a completely worthy value and feeling we can all benefit from striving for, is a feeling often determined by *external* factors. More often than not, it's triggered by people, places, experiences, thoughts and successes. Joy, on the other hand, is experienced *internally* and is defined as a feeling of great pleasure. It is cultivated from within when you can be at peace with who, why and how you are – aka when your vibration is aligned.

In his book *Power vs Force*, Dr David R. Hawkins introduces us to the Scale of Consciousness. From low to high, the levels of consciousness are as follows: shame, guilt, apathy, grief, fear, desire, anger, pride, courage, neutrality, willingness, acceptance, reason, love, joy, peace and enlightenment. Where you sit on this scale changes depending on what is going on in your life, but most of us – at least the people seeking personal growth of some description – will sit somewhere between courage and reason. The higher levels of love through to enlightenment are reserved for a much smaller percentage. You'll notice joy sits higher than love on the scale.

Exercise 3

THE LIFE-CHANGING MAGIC OF TIDYING UP (YOUR VIBRATIONAL FIELD)

You know that feeling when you clean the house, throw a bunch of shit out and you sit down afterwards and feel a sense of achievement – almost as if a weight has been lifted off your shoulders? The energy shifts, you start to feel emotions of peace, love and, dare I say it, joy? Great! Let's do this to your life.

What are the top five things, people and experiences in your life that bring you pure joy?

Remember, joy is a feeling of great pleasure and happiness, and according to Hawkins, it sits higher on the scale of consciousness than love. Because, let's be honest, we can love things that do not (or no longer) bring us joy.

1. _____

2. _____

3. _____

4. _____

5. _____

>>

35

>>

The goal here is to not get rid of everything that isn't sparking joy, because laundry and taxes and all that have to stay. But there will definitely be things in your life that pull you so far away from joy and so far out of alignment with your personal vibration that it might be time to organise a council pick-up.

On a scale of one to ten, where ten equals pure joy, what things, people and experiences in your life have you sitting below five?

1. _____

2. _____

3. _____

4. _____

5. _____

According to Hawkins, it is the advanced spiritual teachers and saints who sit on the level of joy on the scale of consciousness, but don't let the fact that you're not Gandhi put you off striving for joy.

As far as values are concerned, joy is something that we are able to strive for and we can use to guide us, much like Kondo suggests, by asking ourselves if this person/experience/life choice brings us joy. And if it doesn't, well, you know what to do. Bin it!

Now of course, we'd be living in a utopian world if I were to suggest that you should strive to experience joy in each and every moment, but on a scale of one to ten, does X make you feel closer to joy or further away from it?

The compromising conundrum

Now that you know what your values are, it's time to evaluate which ones you're willing to compromise on. I'm not exclusively referring to relationships here either; we compromise our values for friends, family, work commitments and general life experiences. Heck, we compromise our values all the time with our own well-intentioned choices.

When a value is compromised you feel it on a cellular and vibrational level. Often, aside from the internal knowing, there are physical symptoms. I get a sinking feeling in my heart. Sometimes, it shows up as a lump in my throat. Other times, a stomach flutter – not the good kind. The experience of the value being compromised will often play on a loop in my head. Perhaps for you it's a lot more subtle, but getting familiar with how you feel when your values are uncomfortably compromised is key to keeping your personal vibration not only in alignment but firing!

It's important to acknowledge that you're not perfect (I know. It shocked me, too), and that there are perhaps some values you haven't seen from a different perspective. So compromise is definitely still on the table. What's important before you start compromising on all of your well-thought-out values, though, is identifying which ones you're willing to compromise on. Can you accommodate someone or something else and still feel in alignment?

Perspectives (how they view things), physical traits (like how they look or how they tall they are) and qualities (like kindness, ambition, etc.) are all things you can be open to compromising on. (Sometimes you might need to compromise on height.) Integrity, self-respect and your core values (which you uncovered earlier) are a different story.

This is not to say you have to stand steadfast on the list you conjured up in Exercise 3. You might find that in certain situations and with certain people something that once felt like a priority value doesn't feel so important anymore. This is why it's crucial that a) we know what our values are, so we know if they're up for debate and we can give ourselves time and space to consider them; and b) how it feels in our physical and emotional body when a compromise equals not just an endangered value but a weakened personal vibration, something pulling you out of alignment with your own authenticity.

In Part Two of this book, we'll explore aligning your values with a potential suitor and why prioritisation and compromise are equally important. But for now, just make sure you're very familiar with the following:

- ♥ what your core values are;
- ♥ how you feel in your physical and emotional body when you're in alignment with your values;
- ♥ how you feel in your physical and emotional body when your values are uncomfortably compromised; and
- ♥ the difference between your core values and your preference for traits, qualities and perspectives.

Following your intuition

I'm not going to spend too much time unpacking intuition, how to access it or how to strengthen it because there are plenty of resources out there that are dedicated to helping you do this very thing. But here's a summary – a sort of Cliffs Notes to intuition, if you will.

- ♥ Your intuition is your personal guidance system, often described as a gut feeling or inner knowing.
- ♥ You know when you just know you know? That's intuition!
- ♥ Following your intuition will never lead you astray. So if you're freaking out about the reliability of your own intuition, stop! Trust it always.

When it comes to your personal vibration, think of intuition as a big beefy bouncer who stands watch over said vibration. If you don't feed him, keep him well hydrated and listen to him when he says, 'NUP, not this one,' then it's likely that a few rogue compromises, misalignments and plain-ass funky energies are going to sneak past him and weaken your vibration when you least expect it. And if you ignore him? Well, that's just rude; he doesn't look favourably on this either, especially when it comes to your happiness and love life (he's a real softie).

Let's use dating as an example of ignoring intuition, seeing as that's what we're all here for. Let me tell you I've ignored my intuition screaming, 'Frog, frog, big wart-ridden frog!' at me far too many times to recall. So yeah, I've got a bit of experience in this department ...

Let's say you're on a date. It's going well, but there's something off, something you can't put your finger on. Or perhaps your fingers are all over it, but you want this one to work so you ignore the red flags protruding from their various orifices and continue to smile and cross your fingers under the table. At this point, your personal vibration is already starting to question how this one got past the bouncer that is your intuition. Perhaps you were tricky enough to distract your bouncer. while you told yourself, *You're being paranoid, give them a chance, maybe you're wrong.* And you know what, maybe you are paranoid, but if the big, beefy bouncer is saying to you loud and clear, 'This isn't right', it's very likely he's saving you from another toad.

Sure, there are going to be times when you're completely blindsided, and your intuition doesn't pick up the red flags or misaligned energy. We're all guilty of forcibly pushing an available (round) man into a square hole. And you know what? It's a totally fine and completely normal part of dating. But listening to, honouring and acting from a place of intuition is paramount to nurturing your personal vibration.

Plus, it works both ways: when your personal vibration is strengthened, you can hear your intuition more clearly. When I'm in full alignment, my intuition is as clear as day. When I'm stuck in a confusing, low-vibrational relationship, like I was with Kurt, I struggle to access my inner voice because I'm drowning it out like a child who doesn't want to hear the wise words of its parents – fingers in ears and screaming a loud 'Lalalalalalala!' from the rooftops.

What are you intuitively drawn to?

Dating aside, what types of people, experiences and things does your intuition guide you towards? These things will also be an indicator of what strengthens your vibration. For me, it's nature, interesting conversations, cafés with bookshelves and handmade ceramics, autumnal tones, anything Scandinavian, authenticity, early risers, opinions that differ from mine, clever minds, soft touch, polka dots, crosswords, unusual gemstones and warm beverages. Intuition guides me to these places because they bring me joy (see how it all ties in), and at the end of the day, my big, beefy bouncer just wants me to be happy and learn a few juicy lessons along the way.

Exercise 4

WHERE DOES INTUITION LEAD YOU?

Okay, it's your turn. What types of people, experiences and things does your intuition guide you towards? I'm talking about your higher self, your inner knowing, not the attraction to guys with man buns and tattoo sleeves or the ability to sniff out a gelato bar in any city.

Allow this list to be the things that light you up, that bring you joy and that will ultimately strengthen your personal vibration.

Honouring your natural talents

There is not a human on this planet who doesn't have a natural talent for something. You could be lucky enough to have the voice of Adele or the songwriting prowess of John Mayer. Or perhaps you have a natural athleticism or writing ability or can pick up new languages with ease. Maybe your natural talent is communication and listening. You could be wonderful with animals, have a knack for fashion or just be really good at making the perfect Vegemite toast (heaps of butter and a scraping of Vegemite, FYI). These are the things that you should get curious about. These are the things that your soul wants you to explore and, ultimately, these are the things that play a big role in helping you identify your personal vibration, because more often than not, these natural talents are what will strengthen it.

I have a natural talent for cooking. Yes, I studied it, and yes, I worked in food publishing and as a chef for many years, but cooking is in my blood. I feel it on an intuitive level, and the truth is when I'm in the kitchen for enjoyment purposes, my soul ignites! Cooking really strengthens my own personal vibration, and I used to see this in action a lot when I catered yoga retreats. I spent three years catering yoga and meditation retreats across Australia, and I would spend 15 hours a day cooking breakfast, lunch, dinner and snacks for up to 40 people at a time. The kitchen is the heart of any home, I get this, but through no coercion at my end I would always end up with groups of yogis hanging out in the kitchen having a chat with me (often those chats went very deep very fast).

Exercise 5

YOUR PERSONAL VIBRATION'S GOT TALENT!

There are no judges, no golden tickets, no passes or fails at this talent quest. No, I simply want you to get curious about what natural talents you have and how you might be able to explore them a little more to experiment with how they affect your personal vibration.

Remember, natural talents don't necessarily have to be specific skills; they can be personality traits or life skills that come to you effortlessly. Perhaps you're a good listener, an excellent problem-solver or an enthusiastic organiser and planner, etc.

My natural talents are

♥ _____

♥ _____

♥ _____

♥ _____

I can explore these more by

♥ _____

♥ _____

♥ _____

♥ _____

And yes, many of those yogis were probably just hanging around for food, but I also believe there was a magnetism to my energy in those situations. I was so in my element, so in alignment that without me even trying, people were drawn to me. This is what we want to create for you and your dating life: magnetism!

This doesn't mean that you must have a certain skill and go out and do that in the streets to attract passers-by, but it does mean that you should think about what natural talents you have to fuel and feed your personal vibration so that when you are out and about you're magnetic. Having an awareness of what ignites your soul and then honouring it is probably one of the most beneficial things you can do for yourself. And it absolutely doesn't have to be something that you do every day, and it definitely doesn't have to be something you do for work, but when we have a natural affiliation for a certain thing, I'm sorry, but I just don't think that's random or a coincidence. I think it's there to be explored.

Strengthening your personal vibration

Now that we know what makes up your personal vibration: your personal core values, the quest for joy, your intuition and honouring your natural talents, we know which things will determine the people, experiences and situations in your life that will ultimately weaken or strengthen it.

Again, it's important for me to reiterate this: no one expects you to walk around with a strong personal vibration at all times. The entire point of all of this is to be able to recognise when your natural state, your true self, your alignment, your authenticity (or whatever you feel comfortable calling it) is being compromised. Once you can identify when it's strong, you'll be able to absolutely pull the cord, walk away, delete the texts and close the book on the things that are dulling, dimming and dampening your ability to vibrate at a high magnetic frequency. Make sense?

Honouring your core values and prioritising joy

I didn't ask you to identify your core values so you could stick them on the fridge, feel proud of writing them and then not give them a second thought. I did it so you'd have a reference manual to call on when you're faced with decisions, choices and potential suitors. Once I was clear on my values, I actually found it fun to do a spring clean of my life and figure out which parts of me weren't honouring them, and who and what allowed me to stay true to them.

Over the next few days, I want you to play around with this:

- ♥ Consciously check in with your values.
- ♥ Ask yourself, *Are x, y and z aligned with what I value most for myself?*
- ♥ Ask, *Does this bring me joy?*
- ♥ Ask, *How does my personal vibration feel? Strong or weak?*

This exercise isn't about abandoning everything that weakens your vibration; it's about implementing more things that strengthen it, thereby increasing your self-awareness.

Listening to your intuition

As an experiment, this week, can you listen to your intuition and follow it? Just see what happens. Look back at the list of things you feel drawn to and give yourself permission to explore them. Then reflect back on how this affected your personal vibration. Did you feel more radiant, empowered, authentic and aligned? Perhaps you simply felt more like YOU. Once you and your intuition are on the same team, anything is possible.

Exercise 6

HOW DO YOU WANT TO FEEL WITH A STRONG VIBRATION?

Everything we've explored in this chapter has (hopefully) helped you figure out what strengthens your vibration. But how is it that you want to FEEL with a strong vibration? Feelings are really what fuels our vibrational frequency and, as you learned in chapter 1, they're a primary component of the Manifestation Equation.

Finish this sentence:
When I'm radiating and showing up as my most authentic self, I feel ...

Don't hold back. What are all things you desire to feel, and what's holding you back from feeling them right now? When you strengthen your vibration, you'll find these feelings come to you fairly effortlessly.

Here is a little-known secret about your intuition. It's rarely (read: never) wrong. Your intuition will always guide you to an experience necessary for your growth (whether it's obvious at the time or not).

Natural talents

I asked you to identify your natural talents, so now that you have – star student that you are – can you incorporate more of them into your daily routine? Allow them to fill your moments of boredom or dissatisfaction. Again, experiment to see what opportunities or people are drawn to you when you are honouring the things that light you up.

Apart from feeling wonderful and having superhero-level self-awareness, you're also going to start attracting incredible things into your life. That's just a natural by-product of fine-tuning your vibrational frequency. As a little reminder, the Law of Vibration states

Everything in the universe vibrates on its own frequency, and things with a similar frequency are drawn together.

If your vibration is radiating at a high frequency, can you imagine what you're attracting?!

Walking into a date with a strong personal vibration

I'm going to share a lot of beautiful love stories throughout this book. Some will be mine, some will be from other people, but there will be plenty of positive dating stories to whet your appetite for a delicious dating experience. Unfortunately, this is not one of those stories.

It felt kismet. Kismet, for those uninitiated with the term, is defined in the dictionary as destiny; fate. The date I was preparing myself for had all the signs of universal timing. We'd met on an app a year earlier and had connected from the get-go. We moved from app messages to regular texting, and even though there were lots of common interests, plenty of humorous banter and complete conversational ease, the timing just wasn't right. I had recently packed my life into a storage container and had no known address or any intention of finding one for a few months. A date never really eventuated. I got on with my life and went on a six-month journey trying to find my new home.

My new home ended up being 800 kilometres away from my last one, in a small coastal tourist town. Since arriving in this new home seven months earlier, I had experienced Jack and discovered what it was like to be with someone and still maintain a strong vibration. Then I had been with Kurt, and was quickly reminded how it felt to be with someone and completely out of alignment – ignoring my values and compromising on joy, because someone sexy was available, keen, etc.

After Kurt I needed a breather and a wake-up call. In essence, I needed time to get my personal vibration firing again. So I checked back in with my values, noted where I had compromised on them with Kurt and reminded myself that it was absolutely not worth it, ever. I spent time following my intuition and honouring my natural talents, and I found joy a really easy feeling to chase once I knew what sparked it within me. After a few weeks, as you can imagine, my personal vibration was nice and strong, and I was feeling pretty bloody magnetic! I arrived home from a mid-week trip to the supermarket and received a text. My phone told me it was from Nick. And I thought, *Who the hell is Nick?*

> *Hey, Jordanna, totally random but did I just see you in aisle six at* [insert small coastal tourist town supermarket]? *I've left my job in Sydney and have just arrived in* [insert small coastal tourist town] *to see if it's a good fit. I don't suppose you'd like to grab a drink.*
>
> *Nick* [insert appropriate casual yet flirty emoji]

A quick flick back through our previous texts reminded me who he was. Ah, Nick! The one that perhaps I'd let get away ... Was our timing perfect now? I told myself, *See, Jord, this is what happens when your personal vibration is strong! Universal timings seemingly fall into place, a man that you met 800 kilometres away is suddenly right there in your local supermarket passing you in aisle six. You'll have to tell this story of how you met your husband in the chapter of the book about strengthening your personal vibration. It actually couldn't be more perfect right now. *Happy dance**

Our drink was scheduled for the following evening. I received a follow-up text that night confirming arrangements

SIDE NOTE

On that same day, I also got some wonderful news from my publisher about my first book's success, I found $20 in the back pocket of my jeans and I was having a great hair day. Everything was coming up Jords.

and speaking of his excitement. As I got dressed for the date, I was calm. I felt like a really radiant version of myself. I was confident, it felt easy and as I took one last 'go get 'em' look in the mirror on my way out the door, I felt joy.

Now, keep in mind, I had never met Nick. I had never seen him in the flesh. He, on the other hand, had just watched me choose olive oil from aisle six, and perhaps, let's not kid ourselves, even witnessed me put the ice-cream back in the freezer several times before committing to the calories and being done with it. So yes, of course there was a part of me that was a little terrified Nick wouldn't live up to his profile pictures. But he did. Oh boy, did he. He was handsome as all hell.

The minute he saw me, he smiled from ear to ear, his scruffy blond locks cascading down his salt-kissed face after spending the afternoon in the surf. Suddenly I was nervous, but nerves are normal and should never be feared. I did what I always do and started with a funny story from my day (I'll teach you these sweet moves in Part Three). He enjoyed my story and offered up a cute story of his own. But then the flirtatious giggles began a rocky descent downhill (much like this date).

I'm not going to go into the intricacies of him recounting to me in detail the girl he'd picked up at a local bar the night before. And I won't get into how he ordered a drink for himself without asking me if I'd like another. And I'm definitely not going to mention how he spoke about his dalliance with a stripper at his friend's bucks party, or how he professed that he wasn't sure if monogamy was the answer to a happy relationship. Because even though all of those things are BIG red flags, they weren't even the worst thing about this date.

Within 15 minutes of meeting Nick, my values of respect, equality, trust and integrity were being compromised. I felt my shoulders slumping, my chest tightening, and I began stumbling over my words (because, dumbfounded). My joy was being ripped out of my chest like a sci-fi villain was extracting the life force out of me just when I thought I'd completed my quest.

In essence (and in real time), it was, of course, a lot less dramatic. I disengaged from conversation as Nick talked about almost proposing to his ex-lover (who was also a junkie). I rolled my eyes at the waitress several times as she bore witness to this disastrous date, and at the first opportunity that didn't seem overtly rude (because kindness is absolutely a strong value of mine), I asked for the bill, paid half, even though he'd drunk more than me (details) and went on my way with my vibration (and self-respect) 100 per cent intact.

Now, once you pick your jaw up off the floor, quit feeling sorry for me and decide to hold off deleting yourself from the three dating apps you belong to, why don't we examine this tale and see what lessons and positives we can draw from it.

Because my personal vibration was so strong and clear, I was able to identify right from the beginning that things were awry. Now I get it, you're thinking, *MATE, anyone could see this was a disastrous date!* But I'm only telling you the highlights (or rather lowlights) of said disastrous date; there were lots of moments in between that I would have clung to had I not known the strength of my own vibration. Like the fact that we had lived opposite each other on the same street for four years (kismet), or that we had very similar upbringings and family values. The way he spoke about his siblings and the love he had for his parents. The exciting nature of his free spirit, and the beauty that was his salty grin (but yes, also salty personality as it turns out). He had a great job, our values aligned when it came to money, he had an environmental conscience and he had a wicked sense of humour. But he also spoke down to me, belittled my achievements and talked over my responses to his questions. If the Jordanna of several years ago, who completely lacked self-awareness and was just looking for someone to fill a bunch of gaps in her life, had been on this date instead, she would have taken those red flags, stuck them in her drink and hoped he was just nervous, that he'd grow out of it or, better yet, that she'd be the one to change him.

As I walked away from Nick that night, I called a friend and cried. Not because my heart was broken or I felt defeated, or even because it was yet another fishing expedition where I'd been unable to come home with a prize fish, but because I dodged a fucking bullet. They were tears of sweet, sweet joy.

Being in alignment, being in flow and being strong enough to walk away from a handsome, surfy engineer with a cheeky grin because you're not willing to compromise your own personal vibration is exactly the superpower one requires to find a higher love and become a love magnet. According to the Law of Vibration, things with a similar frequency are inevitably drawn together, but that's not to say a few toads might not cross your path first.

- Chapter 3 -

What's killing your vibe?

As simple as it is to strengthen your personal vibration, it's just as easy to weaken it. And I'm not only referring to feeling a bit shit or uncomfortable, or not quite vibing with a certain person or situation. I'm also talking about feeling depleted and completely out of alignment, like you're going against your gut, your heart and your energy levels.

Often, your vibration will weaken when a value is compromised, but aside from the obvious misaligned value there might be with a lover or co-worker, what other things compromise our personal values?

Social media

Everyone's best friend and worst enemy. Social media is still relatively new phenomenon, causing us to constantly question who we are; what we like; how we should feel, think and act; and when we should have achieved this, that and the other thing, and what makes us relevant.

If I could get rid of social media completely I absolutely would. Although there are many wonderful things about it – connecting with friends and loved ones, gaining a voyeuristic window into celebrity (admit it, you love it), free marketing for business, and let's not underestimate the value of a good meme – the comparison, pressure and constant reminder to do more, be more, have more overwhelms me, big time! Alas, I run an online business and my advertising and marketing all come down to my social media profiles, so instead, I have to manage the way I use it and who I choose to engage with on it. If I don't, I find my personal vibration can spiral to catastrophic lows with a simple ten-minute scroll.

The first part of this book is about identifying what makes you, you. What lights you up, what makes you feel good about yourself, proud of yourself, confident to be the best version of you and not settle for anything or anyone that pulls you out of that vibration. Can you say this about your social media presence? If you can be all of those things and still spend your time on the 'gram, the book, the tikky tokky, the tweet machine or that one with the ridiculous filters – snap talk is it? – then by all means, post away to your heart's content. But if you're being really honest with yourself and you're serious about strengthening your personal vibration, it's imperative that you clean up (rather than eliminate) your social media presence (I'm not crazy!). To do this, ask yourself the following five questions:

1. *What is my intent behind scrolling through social media today? Do I even have one?*
2. *How does it make me feel?*

3. *Am I following accounts of people and businesses that lower my self-esteem and make me feel like shit? If the answer to this question is yes, then unfollow NOW.*
   Or, hot tip, you can just mute them or ask not to see their profile on your feed, which means you're not offending anyone in the process of saving your own goddamn soul.
4. *Am I the kind of person who instantly starts comparing myself to others' highlights reels? FYI, if you are, you're 100 per cent normal.*
5. *Do I post things on social media to receive validation? How long does the high of that validation last?*
   The intent behind posting is just as important as the intent behind scrolling. If you only post to receive likes and comments to make you feel a certain vibration, ask yourself how you could achieve that same feeling in a more nourishing way.

Okay, so now that you have a little more clarity as to your social media 'why' and the feelings that ensue, it might be time to clean up your accounts. Take what works for you, but here are some things I have implemented over the past year that have helped me in a major way.

❤ I turned off all notifications for social media apps on my phone. I deleted the Facebook app so now I only access Facebook when I'm on my desktop computer.
❤ I unfollowed all of the businesses and influencers I had been following for inspiration because I realised they actually made me feel like shit and unworthy.

♥ I muted any friends or family who make me feel the same
way. I felt they might be upset if they thought I had
unfollowed them. (Not worth the drama.)

♥ I really cut down how often I post. As I mentioned, I run
my business through my social accounts so I post more
frequently than I would if I didn't, but I make sure
every time I post there is a clear intent behind it –
I'm not using it as an opportunity to boost my ego
or gain external validation.

♥ I have social-media-free hours of the day. This is super
hard for me because, again, I run my own business and
have very flexible hours, but I try to limit my time spent
on social to three check-ins a day. It's amazing how
quickly you adjust.

Social media might not be the demise of your vibration, but
identifying what is – and then making changes to support
yourself – will honestly be the best thing you can possibly do
for your own vibrational frequency. Let's run through a few
other culprits.

The comparison trap

Comparison often starts on social media, but let's not fool
ourselves into thinking it doesn't happen IRL. Long before we
started scrolling, Theodore Roosevelt said, 'Comparison is the
thief of joy.' And he was right! If you're seeking joy, which we
now know is a vibration worth striving for, then comparison is
truly a stealth hoodlum that robs you of what you desire.

This was a fine line I walked for a while, and it was only recently that I saw how deeply I'd fallen into the comparison trap. Perhaps you can relate. Comparison often starts as inspiration. You see someone who you feel inspired by or aspire to be more like on social media or in real life, and you follow their every move, hang on to their every word. Perhaps you even try to emulate what they do in the hope that you, too, will feel, look or act more like them. But the issue here is that you're only seeing what they're *allowing* you to see. You're likely not seeing the less-than-compelling moments of their existence – the stuff that makes them human – and you're definitely not privvy to their personal vibration.

Fundamentally, what's happening when we slip into a comparison trap is that we're measuring our level of self-worth against someone else, which is not an accurate measure of worth at all. The personal vibration that you have worked so hard to strengthen through your values, intuition and natural talents are suddenly compromised by comparing it to another vibration, which for all you know is completely misaligned and weak.

Saluting the shadow

I kicked off chapter 1 by briefing you on four universal laws and how they relate to manifestation. Now I'd like to throw another one in the mix – one that has much relevance at this juncture, especially when it comes to comparison: the Law of Polarity. This law states that **a whole is made up of two opposites that in turn complement each other into a**

sense of completion. Which basically means that nothing is one-sided.

To break it down further, there is no light without shadow, no yin without yang, no hot without cold and no success without varying degrees of failure. When you see a highlight reel of someone's life, it's not to say that doom and gloom is on its way, but rather to keep in mind that – universally speaking – duality is bound to be taking place. Everyone's life is a mix of ups and downs; you are just bearing witness to one of the ups.

When I published my first book, my life on Instagram looked so freaking enviable. I was a published author, I had thousands of Instagram followers, my book was being shared all over social media and selling out in bookstores. I had just moved to an idyllic beach town often voted the most popular place to visit on the east coast of Australia. I hosted two successful podcasts and had also happened to stumble across an easy, simple, fuss-free romance. Life appeared good. And it absolutely was, I can't deny that. This was the light.

But what people saw wasn't the reality of *everything* I was experiencing; there was a shadow side. I was completely burnt out emotionally, physically and energetically. I was struggling to create a consistent income and barely making rent each week. I had spent the last three years of my life putting my personal life back together and mending what I thought was a broken heart, only to have my heart squeezed tighter than I could have expected and my vulnerability tested over and over again each and every day. I wasn't sleeping, I was drinking way more than my liver was used to, and even though Instagram and my real-life day-to-day conversations were depicting one side of the story, I was barely keeping my shit together. I wasn't being false or lying on social media. I just wasn't sharing the whole story – the pain, the struggle or the filter-free exhaustion that often accompanies life's successes.

I often remind myself of this time in my life. If you are going to compare yourself to others, do it with a little common sense and perspective. A tiny percentage of the people in your world are going to give you the full story, and – hot tip – they're definitely not going to be the people you see on social media. Influencers are a commodity. They are selling a lifestyle, and nobody wants to buy pain, misfortune or exhaustion.

If you as the voyeur (which is essentially all that you are when you're in the comparison trap), bear witness to a story, make sure you're considering all sides of it, even the parts you can't see. Be conscious of playing your part in this comparison dalliance by embodying the full spectrum of your own circumstances. When we can find equilibrium within our lives and embrace the shadow side as willingly as the light, we can gain perspective not only on our own stuff but also the stuff of those we constantly compare ourselves to.

But also, know this: someone else's good fortune should never impact your own vibration. If your vibration is weakened by the strength of someone else's vibration, then it's time to reassess what strengthens yours. Which brings me to my next point ...

External validation

Searching for validation from outside of yourself, be it from people, experiences or successes, is a recipe for disaster when it comes to the frequency of your personal vibration. Trying to protect your vibration from external influences is precarious enough as it is, but when you purposefully turn to the external to confirm, decide or make choices on your behalf, not only are you completely bypassing your intuition, but you're also choosing to ignore, deny and disagree with it. Which, if your intuition was a friend, would not equal a respectful and loving friendship. Amirite?

It's a natural human tendency to want approval and confirmation from your peers. But at the heart of seeking others' approval is the belief that your self-worth and deservedness lie in the hands of others rather than your own. It's easy to witness the holes in this belief when it comes to relationships and in particular dating, which is fraught with insecurity. A lack of self-awareness and poor self-respect can be amplified, and these are, unsurprisingly, symptoms of a weak vibration.

I'll wait for him to tell me I'm worthy. If he wants to see me again, it means I am this, and if he doesn't, it means I am that. It's an energetic shitstorm, quite frankly. At the end of the day, self-validation is the only thing you require. Mark my words, this will single-handedly change the dating game for you. When you can trust and have faith in your own innate ability to decide, answer, choose, approve and validate, well, watch out, world! Strong personal vibration coming through.

Do any of the following scenarios sound familiar?

☺ You've been working your butt off on a big project at work and your boss finally gives you praise. You feel great!

☹ You get home from work and your partner criticises your new outfit. You feel shit.

☺ You post a pic of your bubble bath on Instagram and you get 100 likes. You feel great.

☹ You get one nasty comment on your Instagram post about having too much spare time on your hands. You feel shit.

It's a freaking roller-coaster of emotions when you're seeking validation from everyone but yourself. You turn to lovers, family members and friends because you respect their opinion, but their opinions are based on their own values, and hey, you've got your own set of values, remember? Staying in alignment with those is WAY more authentic than aligning with someone else's. This isn't to say their opinions don't matter or that their advice isn't sound, but I cannot stress enough (especially when it comes to dating) that you need to be able to tune in to your own internal navigation system first – aka your intuition.

When I worked for a big publishing company, I craved validation and appreciation from my superiors. It didn't matter how well I was doing, how many KPIs I was hitting or how many projects I completed. Unless I was told (constantly) that I was doing a good job, I would feel like a failure. It was exhausting. Many of us fall into the same trap when searching for a partner. We wait to be told we're smart, or sexy or sassy rather than owning those traits for ourselves.

I spent my teens, twenties and the early part of my thirties waiting to be chosen by men. Thinking, *When will I find the guy who chooses me? When will I meet the man who thinks I am beautiful, intelligent, maternal, sexy, successful and marriage material?* Until he chose me and validated all of those things, I was none of them.

Waiting for validation isn't unique to me. Societally, it's nice to think that feminism has brought us so far, but let's not kid ourselves. We question a single woman in ways we'd never question a single man. Why is she still single? What's wrong with her? A man's bachelor lifestyle is rarely scrutinised. He *chooses* to be single. The day he decides he wants to settle down is the day he gets to choose the woman who will be his bride.

Do you know how many men I've ended up with who chose me, but when I've broken it down I've realised I would *never* have chosen them? Yet their validation of me was so much more important than what I wanted! Crazy when you write it down and publish it in a book (read: embarrassing AF), but I bet you, your mate Sally, your cousin June and your work wife, Mina, can all freaking relate.

I'm telling you now that finding yourself beautiful, intelligent, maternal, sexy, successful and marriage material (if that's your goal) and then going out and choosing a partner who is worthy of you is not only more empowering, it also strengthens your personal vibration. And, as we learned in chapter 1, the Law of Vibration says you attract things to you that are on a similar frequency. Hello, sexy, intelligent and successful future lover.

At the heart of it, I believe we all seek external validation to satisfy our human desire to be seen. We long to be seen for who we are, flaws and all. We want to be known, remembered, embraced and accepted by others. To truly be seen is less about another's gaze taking you in and more about being felt energetically in your own authenticity; being loved and accepted in equal measures of light and shadow.

Brené Brown, author of books such as *Daring Greatly* and *Rising Strong*, and presenter of one of the most viewed TED Talks of all time, 'The Power of Vulnerability', says that truly being seen requires courage and vulnerability. And I think that this is one of the driving reasons humans prefer to look to the external rather than within ourselves. To be vulnerable is to be exposed, and we are terrified of exposing who we truly are, even though it's what we all desperately crave. It takes great bravery to be real in front of another, but it also takes a lot to turn to ourselves and be accountable for our own actions.

I will explore vulnerability when it comes to dating in Part Three of this book, but in the context of your personal vibration, know that being vulnerable and allowing yourself to be seen is a strengthening of and a testament to your own frequency. It's not permission for your authenticity to be evaluated and critiqued by those witnessing it.

People-pleasing

Now that we're gonna quit looking for validation externally, let's be super careful that we're not instigating such behaviour in other people by constantly being a validator for others – aka our old friend 'people-pleasing'.

People-pleasing is a sly misdemeanour. It disguises itself as a selfless act, but actually, it is an act of low self-worth and low self-respect. It's also – you guessed it – just another form of external validation. Sneaky, sneaky!

You see, people-pleasing often stems from personal insecurity, when you're afraid of being wrong, disliked or disagreed with. Often, it's a person's inability to say no that leads them down the path of constantly trying to please others rather than pleasing themselves. There is danger in this long term, especially when it comes to your personal vibration. If you're always putting everyone else's needs above your own, your frequency is undoubtedly going to be compromised. It's the nature of the people-pleasing beast.

The conundrum with people-pleasing is that sneaky disguise I mentioned. It can fool you into thinking that you're being helpful, generous and accommodating, and all of these things are great when they're coming from a place of high regard and a full cup. But if you're accommodating others in order to belong, feel accepted or gain approval, what you're actually doing is lowering your own self-esteem and level of self-worth, and eliminating any sense of personal boundaries.

I used to be such a people-pleaser, especially during the early stages of dating and relationships. I felt that the only thing I had control over was my behaviour and my willingness to compromise. But compromise is a slippery slope when you're the only one shape shifting to make square pegs fit. You find yourself constantly pursuing validation and approval. Every time you say yes when you want to say no, you're weakening your vibration. Every time you agree to help someone else at the expense of your own energy, sanity or time, you're weakening your vibration. Every time you commit to something that feels completely misaligned with your own values, you guessed it, you're weakening your vibration. So, I ask you, is pleasing others at the expense of yourself really worth the damage to your own vibrational frequency?

Energy vampires

My mother once told me a story about a dangerous group of people who exist among us. They look just like you and me, but they are not like us – they are energy vampires. Although human (and most definitely not the undead), they can suck the emotional energy right out of you. They penetrate deep into your emotional energy field, zap you of all your chutzpah and take it on as their own.

Energy vampires can be strangers, or they can be our friends, family, co-workers, acquaintances or partners. They come in many shapes and, from my experience with many different types of energy vamps over the years, I feel confident in saying that very few of them are sucking you dry consciously. And that's good, because it means that the person with the potential to make real change here is *you*. Often, it will mean limiting your time with them and setting up some clear boundaries.

At this point, you may be envisaging Edward Cullen from *Twilight*, or perhaps Louis de Pointe du Lac (Brad Pitt in *Interview with a Vampire*) and wondering what the big deal is, and I'll allow you to indulge that fantasy for another few seconds, but this is their charm. If energy vampires just sucked you of all your emotional energy you would avoid them at all costs, but whether it's their six-pack abs, chiselled jaw, sense of humour, generosity or luminous diamond-like complexion, there is usually a decoy of sorts that reels you in.

The main calling card of an energy vampire is the way you feel after spending time with them. Again, this isn't exclusive to dating. Vampires tend to take more energy than they give, and this is because their vibrational frequency is usually so low that they feed off yours in the hope that it will raise and strengthen theirs.

I had a girlfriend whose company I enjoyed 65 per cent of the time. We worked in similar fields, we had similar lifestyles and we found multiple topics of conversation to connect on. But whenever I got home from a catch-up with her, I felt like shit. My energy was always flat. I'd feel a little bit depressed and, often, I'd realise that I hadn't laughed or cracked a good joke once in her presence (and I've got a great sense of humour and tell a mean dad joke). I kept spending time with her because we were friends, but when I really started to look at what that meant, it was a lot of me supporting her and her belittling my achievements, putting me down, inviting me into negativity and dismissing my contributions to the conversation. She would walk away feeling heard, held and uplifted, and I would walk away feeling drained, dismissed and depressed. Vampire!

By now, you'll be aware that we're all energetic beings with our own vibrational fields. You've been learning how to strengthen yours and this is very attractive to the people around you who are drained of energy or whose vibration is somewhat weaker.

Let's play 'spot the vampire'

Energy vampires come in various different forms. Perhaps you can identify with some or all of the following (or perhaps you identify as one yourself):

THE VICTIM. They constantly play the victim and act as if the world is out to get them. Your role is to make them feel better. This is a futile pursuit because they're preying on your guilt; they're not interested in ever being anything but the victim. They will often blame others for their own misgivings and misdemeanours.

How to conserve your energy: Don't indulge their self-pity. Limit your time with people who are constantly blaming others for their own misfortunes.

THE PROBLEM CREATOR. You know the type: they thrive on drama and create problems to fill a void or emptiness in their lives. Your role is to solve their problems, but as they're self-inflicted, your attempts at fixing or helping them are futile.

How to conserve your energy: Don't allow yourself to get caught up in their drama. Notice patterns of behaviour and try to be aware of what triggers you to want to help them. Does their behaviour trigger your own people-pleasing tendencies?

THE ALPHA. They love to feel superior and dominating in your relationship dynamic. This usually stems from a place of feeling weak or undermined in other areas of their life, so they assert dominance over you. They've likely targeted you because you willingly play the submissive and agreeable one who makes them feel strong and powerful.

How to conserve your energy: Agree to disagree. It's a powerful technique and it keeps all of your boundaries in place. Your assertiveness will serve both your energy and theirs.

THE NARCISSIST. One day I might write an entire book about narcissists. I am a magnet for a self-absorbed narcissist with a complete lack of empathy. Narcissists are also usually quite magnetic types. They have charisma and charm, and they're masters of subtle manipulation. But they're concerned with one thing only: themselves. Their complete lack of self-awareness and concern for others is not only perplexing but bruising to one's ego. Your role is to fluff their feathers, and often you don't realise you're doing it until they stab you in the back or undermine your generosity. The truth is the only thing that matters to them is them. Full stop.

How to conserve your energy: Abort, abort, abort. Especially in a one-on-one environment. Narcissists really are the ultimate energy vampires. Your energy is not a factor for them. So if you have a narcissist in your life, my advice is to set very clear boundaries for yourself (see page 71), and if you need to interact with them because of work or because you share blood, then having an acute sense of awareness of the type of person you're dealing with is paramount, as is choosing to disengage where possible.

THE OBLIVIOUS. I'd go so far as to say that most energy vampires are oblivious to their energy-zapping ways, but there are a few innocents among them who are really just going through a rough time and need your support. As a friend or family member, I understand your role and would never deny you of this, but it's also important to be aware that you should never have to carry the load or be 'the rock' at the expense of your own energy. What help are you then?

How to conserve your own energy: Encourage them to be self-sufficient, and lead by example by explaining that while you're there for them if they need you, you also need to be able to conserve your own energy stores. Encourage strength and resilience by not always picking up the pieces and asserting firm boundaries (see page 71).

THE ASCENDING STUDENT. This starts off quite harmlessly. Often a high-vibrational being will attract people who want some of what they have. Unfortunately, this can swiftly morph into you constantly offering guidance, wisdom and expertise and receiving nothing in return.

How to conserve your energy: Playing the role of teacher and guide is wonderful and should never be refused if it's something you enjoy, but teachers get paid for the work they do (albeit not enough), and there needs to be a valuable energy exchange. In relationships I ALWAYS play the role of teacher. Now self-awareness has made me realise that I play this role because, in a way, I enjoy it, but often I spend the whole relationship knowing more, doing more and giving more while receiving very little in return. It's exhausting, unfulfilling and, for me personally, extremely unsatisfying. And soon enough this leads to resentment.

In all relationships, be they romantic, platonic, familial or professional, there needs to be an even and valuable energy exchange in order for both parties to mutually benefit. When there is an imbalance it opens up a portal for those energy vampires to creep on in.

Energy vampires are also prone to doing the following:

- ♥ refusing to take responsibility for their own actions;
- ♥ complaining constantly;
- ♥ fishing for compliments and sympathy;
- ♥ judging and gossiping about others;
- ♥ leading with their ego; and
- ♥ taking and never giving back.

Sometimes, I feel 'energy vampire' is too strong a term, but I use it for impact. There will always be people in your life who are harder to be around than others. And when it comes to work colleagues, blood relatives and lifelong friends, you may not have too much choice about their proximity to you. But at some point, you need to take responsibility for your own energy field and make a call about whether or not these people are worth depleting your own vibration.

This could be happening within your relationship, or perhaps you attract vampires on the dating scene, but for now I ask you to just consider anyone in your life who is robbing you of your vital energy and life force. It's not selfish to prioritise your own vibration because it doesn't matter how hard you work on strengthening it if you're exposing yourself to people who are intent on stealing it; in short, you're fu ... ndamentally screwed.

Setting healthy boundaries

Boundaries are going to come in super handy later in this book when we put our conscious-dating training wheels on, but in terms of who you fundamentally are as a human and what contributes to the weakening or strengthening of your vibration, boundaries are where it's at my friend. Picture this:

1. Your beautiful, radiant, bangin' physical body.
2. All around you, you're emitting an energy frequency. This is your personal vibration.
3. Around that are the energetic, emotional and sometimes physical boundaries that you must set in order to keep your personal vibration intact. A protective forcefield, if you will.

It's so important that you work out what your boundaries are. Your boundaries will become easier to identify once you know what a strong radiant personal vibration feels like. Basically, anything that attempts to weaken it should prompt you to erect a boundary in order to protect it.

Boundaries 101

I always like to think of boundaries as the Kevin Costner to your Whitney Houston (aka your bodyguard).

Identify your limits

If your energy is feeling compromised, it is up to you to make the necessary adjustments to protect yourself. Other people aren't aware that they've crossed a boundary line unless you're willing to make it clear to them. When you know your limits, you can take responsibility for how you expect to be treated and what you will tolerate emotionally, physically, psychologically and spiritually. In return, it's important to note that you are NOT responsible for the thoughts, feelings, actions or beliefs of others, or how they react to your boundaries.

Learn to say no

As children we are professional naysayers and then we grow up and feel guilty for refusing to attend, participate or give our all. But by simply saying no, you're setting a clear boundary between what is acceptable and what isn't. You can say no with kindness and tact; it doesn't have to be done with anger or icy undertones. The consent we give or deny when it comes to sex is increasingly gaining much-needed attention, but although undeniably important, sexual boundaries aren't the only ones you're allowed to protect. No means no.

Steer clear of resentment

If you feel resentful of the situation you're in or resentful towards the person you're with, it's a pretty clear indicator that you've crossed a boundary line. I now use resentment as a barometer of whether or not a boundary is set to be crossed. I don't wait until I feel resentful. Instead, I ask myself if doing something is likely to cause resentment. Identifying this multi-layered emotion *before* it kicks in will save a lot of energy. A cocktail of fear, discomfort and guilt, resentment usually shows up when we've pushed ourselves past our limits.

You can give a little without giving your all

Giving someone half an hour of your time over coffee compared to hours of your afternoon or evening will create a healthy boundary for how you're willing to show up for people. The only person who can set that boundary, though, is you, and it really just comes down to clear communication. Often, we set ourselves up for the expectation of giving more because we don't communicate that we're only able to give a certain amount. Mind-reading isn't as common as we would like to think.

Drop the guilt

The biggest barrier to setting clear boundaries is the guilt we feel when we do. But ask yourself, *Would someone with a strong and radiant personal vibration feel guilty about keeping their vibrational frequency intact?* Boundaries are not just a sign of a healthy relationship, they are also a wonderful indicator of your own level of self-respect.

Practise self-awareness

The only way to know if a boundary is slipping and your vibration is weakening is to tune in to your feelings. It's so easy to get carried away with other people's shit and get lost in the chaos that is their drama. This is when boundary lines get blurred. When we're super clear on how our vibration feels when it is strong, we are fine-tuned to any feelings that are pulling us out of it. And, people, I have to stress something here: you will not always be vibrating at a high frequency!

The whole point of having an acute awareness of your personal vibration is so you can check in with it constantly.

Because if you can't identify each time your vibration becomes weakened or compromised, it's likely you'll turn around one day, after its gradual unravelling, and think, *How the hell did I get here?*

The most important thing to remember about boundaries is that you've really got to take responsibility for them and adhere to the boundaries that you set yourself, otherwise they lose all of their weight. When it comes to dating and relationships, I'll often go in with a clear set of boundaries and then because of the aforementioned offenders – external validation, people-pleasing, comparison and so on – my vibration becomes compromised. I lose my sense of self and, before I know it, I'm putting up with shit I'm not aligned with, making compromises I'm not okay with and getting caught in another sticky mess.

Maintaining boundaries is a daily practice, and there are going to be times where your boundaries slip. Just know that it's never too late to prop them back up again. It's never too late to say no. It's never too late to admit that a limit has been exceeded. It's never too late to recognise you're out of alignment and to get curious about how to edge your way back again.

Boundaries are less about keeping the bad shit out and more about protecting all of the good stuff you've cultivated.

High-vibrational health

I know, just when it seems like it's a bloody minefield out there, trying to avoid all the different ways your personal vibration can be weakened, I swan in and throw a handful more at you. But these are ones you have complete control over. The following vibration-dampeners are easy fixes. In fact, giving these a make-over can actually be quite enjoyable.

If you're not looking after your energy on a physical level, it's impossible to make big energetic impacts on a vibrational level. It makes sense, right? I'm not asking you to strive for perfection when it comes to your health, I'd just like to encourage you to think about what you're doing to support and nourish your vitality, knowing that a vital body leads to a vital vibration and vital vibration makes you a manifestation magnet!

I'm not about to give you a list of food and drinks that you should or shouldn't ingest. Surely you know that eating a bag of burger rings or binge drinking several nights a week isn't doing your vibration any favours. I just want you to get super curious about how everything you put in your body makes you *feel*. As an experiment, not as a strict diet regime, can you identify which foods make you feel radiant and vital and which foods zap you of energy and make you feel sluggish? This is going to be different for everyone, so I want you to make this a really personal exploration – keeping in mind that it's not always the foods you think. For example, all green veggies when steamed or lightly sautéed make me feel incredible, except broccoli. Broccoli makes me feel like curling up in a little ball and hiding from the world. Not because I don't like it; I love broccoli, but broccoli does not love me.

Coffee is another great example. I love coffee. Like, so much. It's not inherently bad for you. I only have one cup a day, so I'm not excessive, but although coffee makes me feel amazing from first to last sip, my energy rapidly declines after a couple of hours, and the truth is I end up feeling kind of exhausted, which kind of defeats the purpose. Other people don't have the same reaction to caffeine. Lucky them.

Controversially, I don't react to gluten or wheat, but I do find my energy completely zapped when I eat certain types of nuts, seeds and eggs. Go figure! Often, you'll be told something is healthy and assume it's good for you. But just as we can be a vibrational match with certain people and not others, I also believe we're vibrationally matched with certain plants and animals. Don't just take my word for it, Erin Lovell Verinder, a wonderful herbalist and nutritionist I know, says there is 'no one way to eat or diet that is universal'. Instead, she believes it's 'important to activate your intuition and listen in to your body. You may feel wonderful on a plant-based vegan diet, or you may feel dreadful.' She says supporting high-vibrational health is all about tuning in to what fuels us and makes us feel our best – and that isn't necessarily the same thing as for someone else.

As a general rule, food grown from the frequency of the earth will be more vibrationally charged than a processed piece of junk food. The less processing and manufacturing that has taken place, the better. And yes, of course, organic fruit and vegetables are going to affect your vibration more positively than something that's been sprayed with pesticides, but I'm not here to preach perfection to you, I just want you to get conscious about what makes you feel great and what's making you feel just a little bit shit. You see, if your energy is required to heal your body from inflammation or a food intolerance, that's energy that's not being used on strengthening your vibration and attracting a delicious and delectable lover into your life.

When it comes to feeling vibrationally charged from a health perspective, it's important to talk to a health professional. I recommend finding a naturopath, nutritionist or holistic GP and looking at the following with them:

♥ **The quality of your sleep.** This will greatly impact your vibration. If you're functioning on less than 6–8 hours of sleep, it's going to mess with your energy. So get into bed as early as possible to make sure you're not just getting more sleep but a better-quality snooze.

♥ **The health of your menstrual cycle.** Women are cyclical beings just like everything else that exists in the universe, so if you have a menstrual cycle, it's important that your cycle is functioning optimally. A healthy period is a good indicator that your overall wellbeing is being cared for. If you suffer from painful, heavy or energetically debilitating periods, it's worth talking to a professional and committing to improving your period health.

♥ **Stress levels.** I'm talking about day-to-day stressors here and how you manage them. Do you schedule mindfulness practices like meditation, yoga or nature walks into your calendar? If not, why not? What are you prioritising over your mental health? If you're coasting through life thinking stress and its effect on your body are just part of being human, it's time to sit yourself down (in lotus), my friend. Avoiding energy vampires, refraining from people-pleasing and vowing to stop comparing yourself to others is one thing, but if you're in a constant state of flight or fight, you're directing energy towards survival instead of bringing new and exciting things (and people) into your life.

♥ **When your energy peaks and troughs.** I feel radiant from about 5.30 am until 11.30 am. After that, my energy just starts to decline. I've had to really take note of what I eat, how I move and what I put my energy into during the earlier hours of the day so that I can sustain my energy longer after midday.

This is all stuff to experiment with and get curious about. The biggest takeaway here is that if your energy has to work to protect and heal your body because you haven't been looking after yourself, it's going to prioritise keeping you alive over manifesting new things. So let's nourish, restore and show our physical body some love so that we can expand and nourish our vibrational frequency!

Knowing your personal vibration at its strongest doesn't mean anything less is a weaker you or a less-than-perfect you. Perfect is not the goal here. Having an acute sense of your personal vibration is simply a barometer for your potential, and if you're hanging out consistently in a weakened vibrational frequency, your ability to attract, align and feel worthy of potential suitors (I mean that's why you're here, right?) will surely be jeopardised.

- Chapter 4 -

Turning on your love GPS

I have this girlfriend, Rose, who always subconsciously morphs into the guy she is dating. When I first met her in our early twenties, it was obvious; she dated Jagger, the bass player from a band you've most definitely heard of, and wore band T-shirts and leather jackets only to be left heartbroken by him. Days later, she was seen wearing floral knee-length dresses with white boat shoes and gushing about Simon, a promising lawyer she met while having lunch with her father at the yacht club. In our thirties, Rose's transformations were a little less subtle. Her opinions became extremely right-wing while dating young liberal Paul, but then she quit eating meat and dragged me to braless protests while dating greenie Sol. And then, in a scenario that shocked us all, Rose spent two years solo getting to know herself. She then met and subsequently married Derek, who loved Rose for Rose. Turned out playing the part of Rose was her most rewarding role to date.

Watching a seemingly intelligent, beautiful and capable person become whomever she needed in order to be loved and accepted was a harrowing experience. And although you may feel unable to identify with Rose's chameleon ways, it's a lot more common than you think.

You probably do it and call it compromise, which makes you sound considerate, right? But really, what you're doing is making a ton of sacrifices to make it work and compromising your own sense of identity, and that's not what being in a relationship is about.

Having a strong sense of your own personal vibration is an exercise in self-development. It improves your self-worth, gives you unparalleled self-awareness, and enables you to recognise when you're compromising your values and authenticity.

But perhaps the most valuable thing about having an awareness of when your personal vibration is being nourished and supported is that when you start dating and relating with a potential partner, you can be sure you're entering as your own person. If you're not clear on your personal vibration, much like Rose, you can begin to morph into the other person and take on *their* vibration. Or, worse yet, use their vibration to give meaning and substance to your own. This is a temporary fix. It's often why we feel all kinds of wonderful in the early stages of dating, but soon enough this starts to wear thin.

I touched on the notion of completeness in chapter 1, and on how being a 'complete person' is not an achievable or, dare I say it, realistic goal. My intention is not to make you into a perfect human (although if you know how to make that happen, please do let me know), but for you to ask yourself what gaps you are looking for someone else to fill. Is it possible that you can fill them yourself?

These 'gaps' are not part of your physical body. I mean, can you imagine? We'd be walking around looking like slices of Swiss cheese. Rather, these 'gaps' are part of your energetic vibration, and if you can find ways to fulfil and satisfy them that don't rely on someone else, what will end up happening (which is pretty freaking cool) is that you'll attract exactly the kind of person who has all of those qualities, except it won't matter as much because you've already got that shit sorted.

Let me break it down with some real-life examples. Here are some scenarios about a completely fictional single gal you can perhaps relate to ... Okay, they're about me! Well, who I used to be anyway.

THOUGHT PATTERN 1: I'm terrible with money so I must find a partner who is good with money. Then I won't have to think about it. If I can find someone to make the money, save the money and manage the money, then I won't have to worry about sorting out my inability to manage my own finances. Basically, I'll never understand money so I need someone who can.

But what if ... I learned how to manage my own finances? FYI, I did this. I hired a finance coach, I read a bunch of books, I hired a bookkeeper and I committed to – at the very least – understanding money better, even if I didn't enjoy it. I did this BECAUSE it was an important quality for me in a potential partner. These vibrations of at least having the intention to be better with money rather than throwing in the towel and searching for someone else to take care of it added financial independence to my vibrational frequency, thus attracting the frequency of another's financial independence towards me!

But also ... because I'm now financially savvy(er) and I'm not walking around with a big gaping hole in my vibrational field waiting to be plugged with someone else's money know-how, it is less important to find someone to fix me and more important to find someone who values and respects money the way I now do.

THOUGHT PATTERN 2: I'm not unhappy, but when I find the perfect partner, he will make me so happy because I'll finally have the love I've been searching for and even really shit things will just seem a little less shit. Basically, I need love in order to be happy.

But what if ... I found ways to be truly happy outside of a relationship? That doesn't mean I'll settle for never being in one, but it does mean that my happiness won't rest on whether or not I am single.

Because the other thing is ... would you want the weight of someone's happiness resting on your shoulders? Would you want your potential partner to only be happy because they were with you and not happy in their own right? Um, no way! It's so unattractive when you flip it, right?

THOUGHT PATTERN 3: I want someone who accepts me for who I am so that I can accept me for who I am. Basically, unless someone else validates me I am worthless.

But what if ... you accept yourself for who you are? Because here's the thing, you may think someone else validating you will make you feel worthy, but it has a cap.

Because the other thing is ... unless you can feel worthy in your own right without their approval, what you're feeling is not actually worthiness at all.

This isn't to say we need to be all things at all times, or that people can't come into your life to complement your traits with some of their own. It's merely to highlight that if you can't feel content and capable with your own vibration, it's unlikely the other person you're seeking will make you any safer, happier or worthier. Ya feel me? A girlfriend of mine summed things up perfectly the other day when she said, 'Honestly, I wouldn't want to wake up next to me at the moment.'

This isn't coming from a place of self-hate or low self-worth, she is simply aware that her life (and her vibration) isn't in the right state for her to be merging it with another person's. She needs to feel confident in herself because she finds confidence attractive in others, and she wants to be able to offer that to a potential partner. She longs to attract a partner who is responsible with their finances, yet she is far from that, so she's determined to manage her money better. She wants to attract a conscious, healthy and mindful man, but she has let her self-care practices go completely, so within herself she's feeling none of those things. As she puts it, 'I want the next man I date to be a healthy reflection of me because if I attract the partner I long for and he ends up lying next to the person I am today, I wouldn't blame him for not sticking around.' It's an interesting way to look at the quest for love, but it's something I want you to truly contemplate.

If you want to radiate, land a hot date or find your soulmate, it all starts with your personal vibration. After all, this is going to be what matches with their vibrational frequency. We've spent the past three chapters figuring out what lights you up, what you value, what brings you joy and, on the flip side, becoming super conscious of the things that zap you of energy and vitality.

While many manifestation texts will tell you to figure out what you want and then ask you to vibrate on THAT frequency, I pose the following question:

What would happen if you just focused on radiating as the most authentic version of you?

Warts and all. This distinction is important. I am not telling you to simply love yourself and then someone else will love you, because you can totally be loved by someone before you learn to love yourself. What I'm urging you to discover is what makes you *you* in your entirety: light and shadow, hot and cold, highs and lows, good moods and downright grumpy moods. Can you vibrate on that authentic frequency to attract someone in full alignment with the real you?

For clarification purposes, let's go over this once more. We're focusing 100 per cent on *you*: who you want to be as a person and, eventually, who you want to be in a relationship. If you can enter your next dating experience with an acute sense of self, knowing exactly who you are and what you stand for, I promise you dating is going to be so much more rewarding.*

Scared to develop a really strong personal vibration and then have to go and test its strength by mixing it with someone else's? Don't be scared. Be curious. It's time to awaken your vibration to love.

* Author speaks from much experience.

PART TWO

LOVE NEEDS A REBRAND

Love is a funny, funny thing. I'm still trying to understand it. I feel it daily. Mostly for nature, inanimate objects and soulful experiences, often for others, sometimes for myself, but never without layered meaning. When we're young, love starts out super simple: there's the admiration of a flower, the recognition of a cool new toy, a crush on a kid at school, a heart flutter when your crush compliments you or finds you interesting, the curiosity about what it would be like to run your fingers through Leonardo DiCaprio's locks (in his *Titanic* era), your first kiss (most likely sans Leo). Then, without warning, in what feels like a swift progression, love is suddenly laced with possible rejection, unrequited feelings, explosive passion, cutting words, future plans and broken promises.

For me, love had to be explosive in order to qualify as 'real' love. There had to be drama, passion and constant intrigue in order to keep me hooked. But once I was able to tune in to my personal vibration and what keeps me in alignment, I quickly realised that a love like that was never going to be sustainable for my greater good. This changed the dating game big time for me. It enabled me to redefine love in a way that felt true, not just for me, but for my vibrational frequency. Only when I found someone who connected with that kind of love would I be able to truly (and realistically) maintain my own authenticity and set my intention on a higher love. Because wouldn't you rather feel uplifted, complemented and energised by love than be chasing it, overwhelmed by it or trying to convince someone you're worthy of it? But ...

I am not a simple gal. I am complicated. I have multiple personalities (all endearing). My brain never switches off, my heart is always open and often worn on my sleeve. I am curious and crave information, stimulation and conversation, always. But I also love silence. So much so that I have mastered the art of replacing the sound of someone talking at me with the sound of nothingness. It's a talent! I say one thing and mean another. I mean one thing and say another. I place humour and wit above all other traits but take life and love very seriously. I am an introvert through and through, but you wouldn't know it at first glance or interaction. In fact, you probably have a very different impression of me from the person I am. I contradict myself from one moment to the next, but it's who I am. It's who I enjoy being. And only once I was fully able to embrace the unpredictability of my personality was I able to say, 'Hey, Love, let's stop trying to find a perfect match and just concentrate on creating a love vibration that's true for you – and that will attract someone with a similar frequency.' Because when it comes to the search for love, much like you, I have a list.

I expect my lover to be kind, courageous and honest. He is not threatened by my own successes and can celebrate his success without comparison. He holds space for me as I do for him. He communicates in a way that satisfies us both. He is open to the universe but he doesn't feel the need to follow me to every yoga class, meditation event and breathwork circle I attend. He loves to cook and enjoys being cooked for. He enjoys adventure and rest in equal measure, and honours my own energy levels without judgement or critique ... Shall I go on? I don't think I need to in order to prove my point.

You see, this love stuff is great! Perhaps you have a list of what you desire in a lover that is pages and pages longer than mine. It determines who we are and what we want, flaws and all. A thorough and well-thought-out list requires self-awareness; it highlights our inevitable contradictions and accepts our wounds as gifts and our shortcomings as strengths.

But this list is not love. Sure, it helps form part of your love vibration (which we'll explore soon) but being conscious of what you desire and writing it down is not going to make you a love magnet. (#disappointing) In fact, creating higher love is SO much simpler than that, and it's what we'll be exploring over the next few chapters. First, we have to forget everything we know about love through our own experience, go back to basics and find the pure essence of love.

By the end of chapter 7, you will have created a vibration of love that is radically simple – not masked in story or expectation. Not determined by your past experience or somebody else's. It's going to change the way you date and who you attract. And why not? You deserve that.

- *Chapter 5 -*

'Silly Love Songs', Wings, 1984

This is, first and foremost, a book about love – how we consume it, how we let it shape us, how we strive for it, define ourselves by it and what we'd do for it. The deepest love I've ever felt is for coffee (stay with me here). I've loved many men (okay, three). I've told countless men I've loved them (but only truly loved said three). But I didn't love any of them as purely, as sweetly or as unconditionally as I do coffee. And although this feels like one of the many jokes I've injected throughout this book to bring lightness and humour to an otherwise fragile topic, I honestly believe the feeling of love we have for the things

> **AUTHOR'S NOTE**
> You may have picked up on the fact that this chapter heading is also the title of a love song. Well, there are plenty more of those to come, and for good reason. Some of your favourite love songs could be responsible for your warped perception of love. Read on . . .

that can't leave us, can't hurt us, can't disappoint us and can't seemingly hold our future in their caffeinated hands is really love in its purest form, or at least similar to such a notion.

'100% Pure Love', Crystal Waters, 1998

Love is subjective. That I can't deny. But love in its purest form isn't a swinging pendulum of highs and lows. Although we should allow it wriggle room, love, at its core, doesn't wax and wane, rise and fall or turn from hot to cold. Love is not dependent on external factors, it's not defined by physical attraction, possession, banter or intellect, and its opposite is not hate.

Do you recall the Law of Polarity, which states that a whole is made up of two opposites that in turn complement each other into completion? Well, love is the complete energy – not one of the extremes. There is a wholeness to love, and this is what we chase. That feeling of familiarity, of home, of comfort and safety. We use love as a means of completing ourselves, often assuming that being loved by the right partner will make that last puzzle piece land. But love isn't the missing piece, it's the entire goddamn puzzle.

You see, love, in its purest form, is a state of being. It cannot fluctuate because it knows no bounds or conditions. It is unconditional, which essentially means that no conditions, measures or permanency are placed on it. The love we chase in others and attach meaning, validity and worthiness to is not the pure essence of love. This distinction is so important. Love is how we relate to the world, not how we perceive the world to relate to us, and this – I believe – is where love has gotten lost. We focus so much energy on waiting to be loved that we forget that we are love. And I don't mean that in a hippie dippy, woo-woo way, I mean it in actuality. You *are* love. The search is over, you've *always* been love. What you're really looking for is a love to complement your own, and that, my love, is a piece of cake once you've located a strong personal vibration, which you've done, because star student.

I sense you're not satisfied with this new notion I've just thrown at you: knowing that you're already love. I sense you need more. I hear you! Let's have a look at all the shit we pile on top of love, then strip that back to uncover its pure essence. I think then you'll understand that you've been love this whole freakin' time!

'Crazy in Love', Beyoncé, 2003
(see also 'Crazy Love', Van Morrison, 1970)

We talked about 'falling' in love at the start of this book, and while 'falling' in love definitely borders on the overly dramatic, the romanticism of being madly in love, crazy in love, insanely in love and desperately in love is, quite honestly, cause for concern. Sure, it's only a turn of phrase, I get it, but *real* love – healthy love, the love we all truly strive for – surely shouldn't be sending us all stark raving mad. Just for fun, let's break down the meaning of each word.

Madly – to an extreme or excessive degree.

Crazy – (three definitions, none of them appealing)

1. full of cracks or flaws
2. not mentally sound: marked by thought or action that lacks reason
3. Absurdly fond

Insanely – unable to think in a clear or sensible way

Desperately – in a way that shows despair.

I mean, come on, is that really how we want to describe love? Now I know you're thinking *They're just words. Who do you think you are, Jordanna? The freaking adverb police?* Well, actually, yes I do. But also, they're *not* just words, because words, like everything else in the universe, hold vibrational energy. And, according to the Law of Vibration, we're just enabling a frequency around those words and creating crazy, madly, insane and desperate energy around our perception of love. Gross! What if, instead, we were *sanely* in love, *healthy* in love, *hopeful* in love and *calm* and *composed* in love?

'Love at First Sight', Kylie Minogue, 2002

Oh, isn't it just so romantic to meet someone and know the minute you lay eyes on them that they're the one for you? While I'm sceptical that love at first sight exists, I do believe in love at first energetic exchange. Physical attraction is definitely one of the ways to choose a lover, but of the three men I have truly loved (and to ex-lovers wondering if you're one of the three, if you're wondering, then you didn't make the cut), I wasn't initially physically attracted to any of them (no offence, guys). But I *was* immediately alerted to their energy – or since we're now in the know, their vibration. And that's where I want you to be by the end of Part Two of this book: aware of your personal love vibration so that you can identify it in someone else. Love at first vibe, you might say . . .

Once you can determine what love in its purest and most unadulterated form feels like for you and you add it to your personal vibration, well, not only will you then feel that feeling of 'completeness' or 'home' but you're also going to recognise it immediately in someone else – and they in you, no doubt.

But romantic fantasy aside, sometimes it might take you a couple of dates or even a few months of dating before you get a good read on someone's energy. So if you're not feeling 'it' the moment you first meet, give it a little, would you? This isn't a Hollywood rom-com; you've got more than 102 minutes to explore the potential of this relationship and your energetic compatibility.

'Toxic', Britney Spears, 2003

One of the three men I loved participated in our on-again, off-again saga, which unofficially lasted the better part of a decade. Our love was deep but so incredibly messy and complicated that I could never explain it to anybody. And yeah, at certain periods it bordered on addictive, dramatic, unhealthy and toxic. As crazy as it sounds, it's how I measured love in every relation-ship that followed, and it's something I'm only now growing out of. It was undeniable that we had chemistry, but I was 21 when I first laid eyes on him, and that chemistry was built on a weak personal vibration on both our parts.

I'm not asking you to only seek simple, easy and drama-free love – I'm the last single gal who'd be truly satisfied with that. But it's so important for you to understand that the pure essence of love isn't defined by how passionate your arguments are or your emotional dependency on them. It's also not defined by not being able to 'do life' without the other person (by that I mean life admin, like when to call a plumber or managing a bank account), or how good your make-up sex is because, note to self: although always fun, it's not a reason to start a fight.

Personally, I love a healthy argument. But there is a real difference between having regular fights with a partner and having the odd discussion where you have differing opinions. The latter is healthy, the former is what I thought defined a passionate relationship. It doesn't!

Eventually, I realised that not only was I unable to maintain a personal vibration in that relationship, I wasn't even sure *what* my vibration was. And that, my friend, from now on, is how I lovingly encourage you to determine love.

Ask yourself these questions:

♥ *Can I comfortably be my most authentic*
   self in this relationship?
♥ *Can I maintain a strong personal vibration*
   while experiencing love with this person?
♥ *Is the pure essence of love that I already am,*
   being compromised?

This is not to say there won't be times when you push each other's buttons, or your vibration slips – you're only human. But, on a day-to-day basis, can you be true to yourself and be true to your relationship? Because no psychology or relationship book you'll ever pick up will say that toxic, messy and complicated relationships are true measures of love.

Here's the thing about dating: sometimes it doesn't get messy and complicated until you're in a full-blown relationship. So how do you know in the early stages that you're headed for trouble? YOUR PERSONAL VIBRATION! See, this is why knowing your own vibration so important. Now that you're clear on who you are, what keeps you in alignment and what weakens your vibration, you'll be able to tell in the early stages if things aren't going to work down the track. And, god forbid, if you do get blindsided (it's possible, I've watched *Survivor*), you'll likely catch it early enough because you'll pick up vibrational compromises as they happen and you'll know when it's time to walk away (for more on that, flick to chapter 11).

'The Look of Love', Dusty Springfield, 1967

Over the next couple of chapters, we're going to deep-dive into what the pure essence of love feels like to you, and then we're going to add that information to your personal vibration so you can become a love magnet. But first, it's so important to understand that the meanings and adornments you've been giving to love are not so much pure love as they are lenses through which you interpret the concept of love.

For a very long time, love, to me, looked like a fateful Hollywood tale. Elements of right-place-right-time kismet encounters would be followed by just-missed-him moments. And the story would conclude with an 'I can't live without you' declaration from him, and then a wedding and a pregnancy. Truth be told, my projections of love never really went past that point.

I've gone and given you a pretty clichéd version of love, and maybe it doesn't differ much from yours, but as I said, love is subjective and it looks different to everybody. In the interest of science (not really), I hit the streets and asked some questions. Here are some other ways people expect love to look.

'Love, to me, is simple: stable relationship, happy kids, home-cooked meals and a roof over our heads.'

'Love, to me, looks like the hardest goodbye in an airport or a train station, where love is bursting and two people don't want to be without one another for however long – be it three days or three lifetimes.'

'Love, to me, is an elderly couple walking through a shopping centre holding hands.'

'Love, to me, is a combination of big romantic gestures and invisible little everyday things like leaving enough milk in the fridge for your lover's coffee or changing the toilet roll without being asked because it's important to them.'

*'Love looks like sunset walks on the beach, holding hands
and being rugged up in chunky cable-knit jumpers.'*

All of these are wonderful images of love, and I'm not going to
take any of these away from you, but these are also constructs.
If my idea of love differs from yours, does that mean that we
can never love each other? That doesn't seem fair.

We have to view, feel and shape love in its simplest forms
because otherwise we're just adding extra layers of expectation
and pressure to something that is yet to manifest. We'll discuss
the power of the love stories we play out in the next chapter
(brace yourself) and their ability to create – and in some cases
limit – the kind of love we think we deserve. But first, let's
make ourselves feel a little better by acknowledging that love
has been complicated for, like, ever!

The Ancient Greeks had eight different words for love.
EIGHT! Each describes a different type of love.

1. **Eros** – erotic love
2. **Agape** – selfless love
3. **Philia** – affectionate love
4. **Storge** – familiar love
5. **Philautia** – self-love
6. **Pragma** – enduring love
7. **Ludus** – playful love
8. **Mania** – obsessive love

I can proudly (or, perhaps, not so proudly) say that I have experienced all but one of those loves (still holding out for pragma).

If you think eight words is a lot to describe love, the ancient Indian language of Sanskrit has more than 200 words for love. But, much like the different words to describe them, they are just different spectrums of the simple essence of love. Love is the complete energy. All that other stuff is human interpretation, aggravation and dramatisation.

New York Times bestseller *The Five Love Languages* by Dr Gary Chapman explains that we express and receive love in five different ways, and that if you can understand your partner's love language and recognise your own, that knowledge can transform your relationship. In brief, Chapman's Five Love Languages are:

1. acts of service;
2. words of affirmations;
3. gifts;
4. quality time; and
5. physical touch.

Just as you might prefer chocolate ice-cream while I'm more of a dairy-free lemon sorbet gal, and you might eat your ice-cream out of a cone while I'll always order mine in a cup with an extra scoop, at the end of the day we both still enjoy eating delicious frozen desserts. And that – the enjoyment of the frozen deliciousness – is the essence. The flavours, the style, the types, the amount of lactose might differ, but the experience is what matters. (BRB. Off to get gelato!) Similarly, Chapman's love languages are a means of *expressing* love, they aren't love itself. See the difference?

'The Power of Love',
Huey Lewis and the News, 1985

I hope I haven't scared you off love! I assure you that isn't my intention. I simply want to demonstrate the simplicity of love and the power that such simplicity holds. I'm not saying that any of the aforementioned scenarios aren't love. They absolutely can be. Love is probably the most multifaceted emotion, concept or construct you'll ever experience. But, for the purposes of your personal vibration, I hope you can see why it's necessary to strip it back, if only temporarily.

Our propensity to try to conjure love from something that it's not and force it into self-inflicted storylines, moulds and expectations limits us. The essence of love is not created when we merge with another, it exists inside each and every one of us in our own right. It always has. It's what we do with it, how we express it, receive it, reflect it and abuse it that shapes our experience of love. Without the recognition and awareness of your innate ability to love and be loved, seeking love outside of yourself is simply a band aid.

I've said this before, but it bears repeating: you don't have to love yourself in order for someone else to love you – it is absolutely not a prerequisite to a lasting relationship. BUT if you're seeking a higher love – a love that allows you to show up whole, strong and full – then recognising the essence of love inside of you and adding it to your personal vibration is key.

But before we get there, it's important to be conscious of why you view love the way you do. I shared my belief that unless love was passionately complicated it was not worthy. We all write our own stories then run them over and over again in our heads. And it's imperative that we are aware of what those stories are, where they came from and why it's just as easy for us to write a new story as it is to tirelessly keep playing out the old one.

Chapter 6

Who the f*ck wrote my love story?

We grow up reading and watching love stories, listening to the love stories of others and fantasising about starring in our very own romantic tale. Whether you're conscious of it or not, you're actually the lead in a story you've subconsciously written for yourself. This story influences the way you date, relate and welcome love into your life. This narrative is the lens through which you observe love. Looking through it, you determine what love is and how you expect it to show up. It will also influence the way you give, receive and refuse love.

The problem isn't so much the story itself, but rather the foundations on which it's built. You've most likely based your story on your past experiences with love, other people's experiences with love and what you witnessed growing up at home, on TV, in the movies or in your favourite novels. Or perhaps, your story is based on nothing at all, and is merely an assumption or a prediction. Either way, it's almost always a reflection of what you believe you deserve. The problem with these love stories we subconsciously play on a loop is that the lines often get blurry. We forget that our stories are simply thoughts. And, as I mentioned in the very first chapter of this book, it's estimated that a whopping 85 per cent of our thoughts aren't even true, yet they form our beliefs. Subconsciously, your thoughts are penning your romantic future, and they're not even true!

I've always had a very romantic, idealised version of love. When I think back to my first crush at about nine or ten, I distinctly remember lying on my bed in the afternoons after school and fantasising about the different ways he would confess his love for me. I'd read magazines like *Dolly* and *Girlfriend* (which, in hindsight, I probably shouldn't have been reading at that age) and imagine my ten-year-old self having the kind of relationships and love-fuelled feelings reserved for the older teens in the pages of those mags.

At the age of 12, I developed a crush on a boy called Eros (no joke, that was his actual name). I was away on a family holiday on the South Coast playing the Hanson Christmas album on repeat through my red Sony Walkman (yes, it was on cassette). Again, I was fantasising about Eros showing up on the doorstep of our holiday home with a bunch of flowers and confessing his love. Two years later, at 14, I was introduced to and subsequently became obsessed with the teen angst drama *Dawson's Creek.* I longed so badly to have grown up in a small town, so much so that I used to get angry at Mum for my big-city existence. I wished that I was like the characters in the show, tangled up in a confused and muddled relationship like that of Joey and Dawson, or Joey and Pacey or Jen and Dawson or ... well, you get the picture.

There's nothing extraordinary about the way I viewed love as a pre-teen/teenager. My experiences are probably similar to those of countless other kids growing up all over the world. But what I realised as I entered my thirties was that I was still holding out for much of that idealised version of romance. I found myself waiting for grand gestures, small-town romances and brief yet flirtatious conversations with strangers that would lead them to conduct a thorough investigation into who I was, where I lived and what I loved. Finally, they'd track me down months, perhaps years, later and declare that they'd never stopped thinking about me. I can sometimes allow myself to fall so deeply into the romance of what is essentially scripted love that I stop being active in my own life (read: not dating) and just wait patiently on my couch for my destined lover to rock up.

Other times, I swing to the other extreme and become super realistic in my pursuit of love. During these moments, I find myself detaching from fantasy and magic, and viewing love through a really 'achievable' lens. But is this any more fulfilling? And is there anything intrinsically wrong with indulging in a little fantasy? We'll explore that soon enough (although I'm not sure my answer is conclusive), but first, let's look at what shapes these stories we tell ourselves about what love should look like, feel like, be like.

You are not your parents

I'm not a psychologist, so we're not going to have a 'take a seat on my couch' moment. I can't possibly attempt to help you identify every misgiving you have due to your parents' ability to love each other (or you) too much or too little. I simply want to bring awareness to the fact that the love (or lack thereof) you witnessed from day dot on this earth has likely impacted the way you view, experience and act out love. And, subsequently, it has also shaped the story you tell yourself about love.

At the same time we're being taught to brush our teeth, use the toilet and count to ten, we're also inadvertently picking up on the way the adults around us converse, listen, express emotion, show affection, handle intimacy, navigate conflicts, exercise autonomy, trust each other *and* maintain relationships.

The relationship between our parents (or primary caretakers) is our first experience of observing love in the wild. We are their impressionable audience, and we witness

- ♥ the love they have (or don't have) for each other;
- ♥ the love they have for us;
- ♥ how they receive the love we give them;
- ♥ the way they let us love others; and
- ♥ the way they choose to communicate
  with us about love.

Sometimes, the story you tell yourself about love will mirror elements of their relationship, or perhaps the story feels purposefully different to the narrative that played out when you were growing up. It doesn't much matter, both are valid. Having self-awareness about the fact that perhaps some of your misconceptions, misgivings or fantasies about love are not actually your own but somebody else's is the first step to revealing your current love story.

ROGER AND ANNIE: ONE STORY, TWO LENSES

In 1945, post World War I, June, a matron of a hospital, met her husband, Jimmy, a radio announcer and jazz musician, at the party of a mutual friend. They formed an instant connection and in a state of euphoria and gratitude for every connection and every heart flutter, they married after six weeks. Their love was strong, but their differences were many. After a couple years of enduring Jimmy's bohemian lifestyle choices, June lovingly encouraged him to study medicine and take up a meaningful and well-respected profession. Jimmy complied because he loved June, and he became not only a doctor but also one of the best in his field. Many years later, June and Jimmy had two kids, eight years apart.

Their son, Roger, grew up to be a successful writer with an interest in the bohemian lifestyle his father had left behind. He thought marriage was a ridiculous notion, and always believed that his mother had steered his father away from true happiness. He vowed to never allow a woman to have the same influence over him.

Their daughter, Annie, saw love through a very different lens from her brother. Her parents' love story sold her a romantic and feasible way to fall in love, and this subsequently became her biggest hurdle. She believed, after hearing her parents' story several times throughout her childhood, that meeting someone and knowing after just six weeks that you could spend the rest of your life with them was absolutely the indicator of the potential of a relationship. She soon came to realise that it was not. She grew up admiring her mother for being the kind of woman to recognise the potential in her father and encouraging him to realise that potential. Annie found herself always searching for the potential in others in order to achieve relationship success.

Two children, raised in the same household, both walk away viewing love through very different lenses. And both walk away playing out their own relationships through these subconscious filters of what love is. Is either correct? Is either healthier or truer than the other? Doesn't much matter, but it's interesting to see how one story can play out in different ways.

I grew up as a child of divorce. And not just one divorce, but several. My parents have both been married more than once. Now that I'm an adult, I can see reasons for each of those divorces, and I respect their ability to take action when something wasn't working. Unhappy marriages, unfortunate circumstances and growing apart. Given this history, you'd think, and I reckon most psychologists would concur, that I'd be pretty terrified of getting married. But I'm not. I'm not even scared of getting married and then getting divorced. I was not traumatised by their divorce; to be honest, it's the only thing I knew. Dividing my time between two parents was normal. In fact, it was more normal than growing up in a household of two parents who were still together. I'd never experienced anything different.

However, because of this history, I probably don't view marriage as seriously as I should. Whereas some people might feel that marriage and babies mean forever, I am under no such illusion, and this has proved a pressure point in some of my relationships. I am convinced that no matter how much someone says they love me, they could leave at any time, and, consequently, that exact scenario has played out several times. But the whole point of being aware of this stuff is so that you have the option to steer your relationship choices in a different direction.

Although my parents split when I was three, they never spoke a bad word about each other (to me anyway), and they've maintained a very amicable and mature relationship with one another for the past 32 years. They've both always expressed love openly to me, and I never leave an engagement or a phone call with either of them without exchanging I love yous. I believe this is one of the reasons I find it very easy to tell partners I love them (even if sometimes I'm probably not 100 per cent sure I'm IN love with them). It feels natural, normal and polite to do so. It's a familiar and direct way of letting someone know how you feel ... or so I thought.

I cannot tell you how many guys I've dated who've told me that their parents never said 'I love you' when they were growing up. And I'm not even talking about saying it to each other, I'm talking about to them. This shocked me! Mum told me she loved me every chance she got, and I've never hung up from a phone call with Dad without saying, 'I love you' and expecting to hear it in return. But this stuff is important to consider when looking at the way you view love. Of course, how your parents displayed it, voiced it and spoke of it will influence how you perceive it and in turn give it. It makes sense that these guys didn't feel that saying 'I love you' meant they loved me any more than if they didn't. 'Of course I love you. Just because I don't say it doesn't mean I don't mean it.' Hmm. This took some processing for me, but I see their point.

These examples and stories are all to help you to see the significance of whatever it is you subconsciously took on while growing up. I'm not here to point fingers at your parents and neither should you. That's not the point of this chapter. You're simply, gently, lovingly peeling back the layers of the story you've created for yourself. The good news is that you absolutely get to write a new one that supports, nourishes and uplifts you and your love life.

VIOLET: FLIPPING THE SCRIPT

Violet grew up with hippies for parents. They were madly in love ('madly' being the operative word). Her mother was an alcoholic and her father liked to smoke all of the weed. The love they had for each other was kind of toxic, and even through Violet's pre-pubescent lens she could see how addicted they were, not just to their vices but to each other. When Violet was 16, her parents separated. She and her two siblings split their time between two households. When they were at their mum's place, Mum would talk shit about Dad. When they were at their dad's place, Dad would probe them for details about who Mum was dating. Sometimes they would come home from school and see their dad's car in the driveway and find their mum standing in the kitchen in her robe making him afternoon tea. This was not the kind of love Violet wanted for herself.

When she was 18 and fresh out of high school she met Chris. Chris was a catch. He came from a pretty cookie -cutter family. They ate meat and three veg most nights. Violet found a stability and love in Chris that she'd never had at home. It felt unfamiliar but so very right. After eight years of dating, they got married, and they've been together for 12 years now. Their marriage is built on trust, communication and deep respect. Violet consciously built a relationship that was the direct opposite of the relationship she grew up in the middle of.

Your parents might shape your love story, but they don't define it.

Exercise 7

YOUR LOVE ORIGIN STORY

It's time to unpick how love was demonstrated, communicated and expressed at home when you were growing up. Now, the most obvious place to start is with your parents, but your grandparents or any other adults that you spent a lot of time with may have also influenced you. Remember, no judgement, we're just making observations at this point.

I've written some questions to start you off and get you thinking, but because families come in so many different forms these days, these questions won't suit everyone's circumstances.

>>

>>

So I'd like you to freestyle it a little here. If your parents were divorced and remarried, you might also like to include your step-parents in this story.

Write down the ways you experienced love growing up. Contemplate the following questions:

- ♥ Were your parents together?
- ♥ How did they express their love for each other?
- ♥ How did they express their love for you and your siblings?
- ♥ Was everyone treated equally in the household?
- ♥ How was love spoken about at home?
- ♥ Were you able to talk openly about relationships at home?
- ♥ Were there open displays of affection?
- ♥ Do you know how your parents met?
- ♥ Did you feel like you had to prove yourself to them in order to receive love?
- ♥ Did you need to be told you were loved in order to feel validated?

Now that you've started digging, you may find that memories start to creep back in over time – these may hold clues to why your love story is the way it is. Write them down as they surface. Get familiar with each and every one of them, so that you're able to set yourself free with the next exercise.

Exercise 8

LETTER HOME

Write a letter (or letters) to your parents (or caregivers) voicing any feelings about how love was represented at home when you were growing up. Anything that you feel would be helpful to get off your chest goes in this letter. You might like to thank them for certain things and ask them why they didn't find other things important. However the letter-writing goes, tell them that you forgive them and that you are no longer defined by the example that they set. You are your own person. And you have chosen to write a new love story.

DO NOT SEND THESE LETTERS!

You are not what you watch

I don't think there's a single Hollywood romantic comedy that I haven't seen (it's likely I've seen them more than once). I know this because I check the new releases on iTunes every couple of months so that one doesn't pass me by, and I visit every BuzzFeed, IMDB and Rotten Tomatoes list of the 'best rom-coms you've never seen' on the reg. I'd like to say I don't know what it is that I love about them, but that would be a lie. I know exactly what it is, and it's likely the same reason you love them, too. It's their mixture of real-life moments (giving them just enough relatability) with hope and fantasy (which provides the escapism). They give a sweet taste of potential and possibility, followed by a montage of super romantic (often unrealistic) moments, while conveniently leaving out the everyday shit that makes dating and relationships hard!

I was trying to think back to the first romantic comedy I ever watched and soon realised I've been watching them since I was old enough to be distracted by television. The first romantic comedy I remember watching on repeat was *Lady and the Tramp*. If you need a reminder of the plot it goes something like this: Lady, a pampered cocker spaniel (think Charlotte from *Sex and the City*) finds her comfortable life in disarray when her owners have a baby. Lady finds herself out on the street lost and confused, and she's befriended by a stray mutt from the wrong side of the tracks called Tramp (a canine version of the Colin Farrell type – to this day I still find myself attracted to Tramp-like men). A romance begins to blossom between the two, but their many differences threaten to keep them apart. Thankfully, adventures and rescues ensue and . . . they end up living happily ever after with a cute litter of little puppy replicas of them both. Naaawww!

Honestly, replace the dogs with Kate Hudson and Matthew McConaughey and you've got yourself a rom-com you've seen a million times before. A chance encounter, an unlikely friendship, a bunch of adversities and a happy ending.

The Little Mermaid? Rom-com. *Sleeping Beauty?* Rom-com. *Snow White?* Rom-com. *Beauty and the Beast, Aladdin, Pocahontas, Cinderella* ... shall I go on? Could Disney be responsible for our warped ideal of romance?

Do you know what the winning formula of a rom-com is, Disney or otherwise? And do you know the reason we've developed an obsessive addiction to them? They make us fall in love with love, but an unrealistic representation of it. And this is actually a really big problem when it comes to our expectations of dating and relationships. If you could watch the movie and separate the fabricated and over-produced love from real-life love, it wouldn't be an issue. But, if you're completely honest with yourself, you'll likely realise there is no real distinction, and this could not have been made more apparent to me than while researching for this chapter.

In 2008, relationship experts at Heriot Watt University in Edinburgh studied 40 top box office romantic comedies made between 1995 and 2005 (the golden rom-com era). They found that the problems typically reported by couples who came for relationship counselling at their centre reflected the misconceptions they had about love and romance thanks to what they'd seen depicted in Hollywood films. They didn't screen any Disney films, but I bet you it would have shown the same results. But wait, it gets worse (and more embarrassing for me). The films included *You've Got Mail*, *Maid in Manhattan*, *The Wedding Planner*, *While You Were Sleeping*, *Notting Hill* and *Four Weddings and a Funeral*. I've seen them all several times and honestly consider them some of the best films ever made (wait, that's not the embarrassing bit). As part of the study, 200 student volunteers were asked to watch a movie. Half had to watch the 2001 romantic comedy *Serendipity*, the other 100 watched a David Lynch drama (yawn).

I've always loved *Serendipity*. It's a cute film set in New York City with the also cute John Cusack and Kate Beckinsale. But after reading the aforementioned study, turns out my propensity to believe in fate, destiny and kismet encounters was spawned at the very impressionable age of 18, on the very day I sat down to watch that movie in a Hoyts cinema – popcorn and choc-top in hand.

Just like me, the students watching *Serendipity* were later found to be more likely to believe in fate and destiny. And a further study found that fans of rom-coms were more likely to believe in predestined love. Don't you hate when you're just like every other impressionable mind out there (or, at the very least, exactly like the 100 volunteers who took part in the study)?

I actually remember feeling disappointed that my very wonderful and loving boyfriend at the time had only started dating me because I asked him to my school formal, and that our love was in no way predestined or forever (turns out I was right). This was only made even more evident after I (and 100 volunteers) were brainwashed by the very cute, very quaint, in no way threatening, although turns out extremely influential movie about New York City, destiny and a $5 note, *Serendipity*!

This whole time, I've been shaping my idea of romance and the love story I run over and over again in my head in the same predictable way as millions of other people – so much so that 'serendipitous' became part of my vernacular to describe fateful encounters with potential lovers. (I cringe at my easily influenced predictability.)

While I'm not about to tell you to stop watching romantic comedies (I would NEVER), it's worth noting that if you find yourself subconsciously waiting for a Prince Eric to cure you of mermaid-itis, or a Harry to deliver a grand monologue detailing the many ways he loves you after years of back and forth, or for a Hollywood actress to stand in your quaint English bookstore and ask you to love her, then it might be time to ask yourself if this is a realistic way to measure love.

Exercise 9

A HOLLYWOOD ROMANCE

On some level, I think we're all heavily influenced by the love we've witnessed in movies, on TV or in our favourite novels. Again, I don't think there is anything intrinsically wrong with this. However, there are rules we place on ourselves, expectations we place on others, and disappointments that we encounter when we feel that our lives haven't lived up to the imagination of a script writer, director, producer or novelist.

Can you think about some unrealistic expectations you place on love that have been influenced by the world of make-believe?

You might like to contemplate the following:
- ♥ the plots of your favourite movies or books that you've hoped your own love life would mirror;
- ♥ specific characters that you idolise in terms of romance or use as an example of how a lover should behave; and
- ♥ the story threads that you gravitate towards.

Ask yourself if there is a pattern here. Can you see your own love story reflected in any of the above?

You are not your past relationships

With each new partner, I often wonder how the relationship would play out if we were each other's only experience of love. What if neither of us had past wounds, trauma, broken hearts or triggers? Would the relationship stand a greater chance if we weren't both rocking excess baggage? Imagine if all we were allowed to arrive with was a very lightweight carry-on, full of hope, innocence and an open heart. How good could that relationship be?

We'll discuss what's happening from an energy perspective when it comes to baggage in Part Three of this book, but for now, I'd like to focus on the impact that past experiences of love have on the way we pen our love story moving forward. It'd be naïve to think that anything you experience in life wouldn't impact a similar experience in the future. After all, we're taught to learn from our mistakes, and there is validity in that. But often, what ends up happening is that we place expectation on a new experience based on the way the previous experiences have played out.

I've always dated men who pursue me, chase me, beg for me to love them until I give in. It's this weird pattern I got into at the age of 19. A man would chase me tirelessly (this made me feel worthy and validated), I would refuse his advances (this gave me the power), he would be persistent (in a decent and consensual way), declare his undying love for me and I would then soften. He'd be thrilled, I'd eventually let down my walls completely because he'd shown me I was worth fighting for, and then slowly, over the next few months, the power dynamic would shift and I'd be left broken-hearted.

It all began with Charlie, a boy I tirelessly chased. He wasn't much interested in pursuing a relationship with me but after enough convincing on my part, he gave in. We dated for a little while, but he instantly made me regret my pursuit because, truth be told, he was a bit of an asshole, and he treated me the way you'd expect an asshole to treat someone: not well. After that relationship, I swore I'd never chase anyone ever again. If I was going to date someone, they'd need to do all the hard work and let me know they were interested in me. And what do you know, that's exactly the type of guy I started to attract. I'd crafted this very detailed story about how love would play out for me, and part of it was that that love would only last if someone proved they actually wanted to be with me. Thus, I always attracted the type of partner who was purely in it for the chase.

MANDY AND JENNA: TOO HOT TO HANDLE

For many years, Mandy had a rule that she lived by: never date women who are better looking than you. Jenna was her first serious girlfriend, and next-level stunning. Whenever they went out at night, Jenna would always get picked up at the bar, by both men and women. Although Mandy didn't deem herself the jealous type, and trusted Jenna completely, she did find it uncomfortable. I mean, who wouldn't? Jenna always brushed it off, promising she would never take anyone up on their advances, until the one night she did. Mandy was away, and Jenna had a one-night stand with a woman she'd met at the bar. She swore it meant nothing, but Mandy's trust had been broken. From that point on, Mandy associated good looks with cheaters. She'd created a story in her head that should have been reserved just for Jenna but was instead now attached to any woman who could potentially draw too much attention.

MARK AND SUSAN: THE KIDS ARE (DEFINITELY NOT) ALL RIGHT

Mark fell in love with Susan, a single mother with three children. He loved everything about Susan: her fierce opinions, intelligent wit, beautiful smile and the love that she had for her kids. After four months of dating, Susan invited Mark over for dinner to introduce him to her little ones. It didn't go well. Nine-year-old Marley locked herself in her room. Seven-year-old Sam refused to talk to Mark, directing all questions to him through his mum. And five-year-old Ria hid under her mother's skirt the entire night.

The next day Mark called Susan to thank her for dinner and to acknowledge the significance of introducing him to her children. Susan didn't answer. She didn't answer when he tried the next day, or the day after that. The following week, he received a text from Susan that read, *I'm sorry, I thought I was ready to introduce the kids to a man that wasn't their father, but it's too much, this is too much.* Mark offered to slow things down. He said he'd support her and the kids in any way they needed, but Susan had made up her mind. Mark vowed to never date a single mother again.

These stories are true, and I'd hazard a guess that they're pretty common and perhaps even similar to your own. Replace 'better looking' with 'more money', or 'single mother' with 'business owner' depending on your experiences. The point of these tales is not the specific experience itself, but the fact that each story (including my own) illustrates how using the outcome of one experience to predetermine how a completely different experience, with similar yet totally different components (read: people and circumstances), might play out. Half the time, we're not even aware that we're doing this, but it's adding false credibility to our love story, so this is the day you put a stop to it.

Other past-relationship experiences that might affect the current love story you're running include) but are not limited to) the following:

- ♥ childhood crushes;
- ♥ first kiss, first love, first heartbreak;
- ♥ your first serious relationship;
- ♥ losing your virginity;
- ♥ being embarrassed, disappointed or rejected; and
- ♥ any kind of abuse, physical or otherwise. (If this is you, please seek professional advice. This kind of trauma goes beyond the scope of this book.)

As you might have suspected, shit is going to get real in this chapter. I'm going to ask you to pen your current love story by diving deep into some serious self-awareness about your parents, your past relationships and, yes, your propensity to use your favourite romance novels to determine what constitutes love

(*The Bronze Horseman*, anyone?). Once you're clear on all of that, we're going to get some closure on childhood triggers, grudges you hold against how love was portrayed in your youth, and every little piece of baggage you've picked up along the way from first pash to last dash by healing them. In Part Three of this book you're going to be dating (well, I'm going to teach you some things and hopefully you'll put them into practice), and you don't want to use your past stories as an imprint of what you should expect to experience with new partners. Before you dive into a new love scenario it's so important to have healed from the last one.

Time to throw out that 'perfect partner' checklist

Whatever state your current love story is in, it's highly likely that it's the reason that you're still single. You see, when we tell ourselves these stories over and over again about what we deserve, who deserves us, what love will feel like and look like, we filter out anything that doesn't fit that vision.

At the start of Part Two, I mentioned that most of us, at one time or another, have written a list of our future partner's ideal traits and attributes. And while being clear on what you value in a partner is important (and we'll look at that in the next chapter), many of us are using these lists to form a very tight perimeter around the kind of lover that we'll accept, and anything outside of that we instantly dismiss. Soon, I'm going to invite you to craft another type of list, but for now, I want you to throw out the current one. You have no idea what kind of love you could potentially be missing out on.

CARRIE AND MIKE: RUNNING AWAY FROM MR RIGHT

Carrie (no, not that Carrie) found dating exhausting. And it was easy to see why: she loved the chase (common story, it seems). She loved having to prove herself to potential partners. It felt like a challenge, the good kind, and it kept things interesting. But boy, was it hard work. When she met Mike on a dating app, he liked her straight away and it scared her. She found herself thinking, *What's wrong with him? He's so clingy!* She didn't need to impress him, and although that seems like a dream scenario, her modus operandi was convincing men that she was great. This guy seemed too easy. Plus, there was a bunch of boxes he didn't tick: Mike was from another country, so she didn't really see how there could be a future in it; he was an introvert and Carrie only dated extroverts; he wore his heart on his sleeve whereas Carrie was used to dealing with hearts that were locked up in steel boxes and then securely fastened with thick chains and oversized locks.

Carrie did enjoy spending time with Mike, though. He was funny and sweet and she also found it easy to let her walls down with him. So, Mike got friend zoned. Carrie continued to date, to chase and be chased, and her friends and mother would lovingly nudge her back towards Mike. 'The perfect guy is right there. What is wrong with you?' they'd say. But Carrie convinced herself of her type long before they met and had an idea of how her love story would play out, and Mike didn't fit the narrative.

It's easy to see that Carrie was blind and Mike was a catch when you're on the outside looking in, but this is the power that our stories hold over us. They blind us, shield us, and allow potential partners to pass us by. I'm going to fast forward Carrie's story a little. Mike is now her fiancé. The traits of his that Carrie initially dismissed as thirsty, clingy and too available were, in fact, open, honest and kind. And the chase that Carrie thought defined love was, in fact, just a means to make her feel validated, which she never ended up feeling in the long term. Once she was able to drop the story of how love should look, she was able to truly allow herself to experience the kind of love worth saying 'I do' for.

Exercise 10

THIS IS A SHOUT-OUT TO MY EX

Okay, I get that this exercise is gonna feel super icky. But boy is it necessary. We're going to bring awareness to all the stuff you're carting to every relationship and then you're going to go through each one of them and find closure. Like, proper closure. This is a game changer, friends. I repeat GAME CHANGER!

You might be wondering what defines a 'relationship'. Let's start with everyone you've ever had a crush on, pashed, dated, had a one-night stand with, or had a short-term relationship or a long-term relationship with. Nobody is going to pass us by. If you don't remember them, it's unlikely they impacted you greatly, so move on. For some of you, that might be one person, others might find themselves in the triple digits. Some of these people will have had zero impact on you and we can move past them at top speed. Other people are going to bring up some shit, but don't let that stop you. Take your time. Be thorough.

The process:
- List your past experiences one by one.
- What impact did this relationship have on you?
- Do you still think about that person? If so, in what context?
- Do you hold resentment towards them? If so, why?
- Do you still hold a flame for them? If so, why?
- Have you taken baggage accumulated in this relationship into subsequent relationships?
- If you had to describe this person in three emotions, what would they be?

If this exercise triggers you, please call a friend or family member, NOT someone from your list. We're wrapping these relationships up, not reopening old wounds. From this point, we're going to be forgiving and healing, and this can absolutely be done with zero contact with them. I'm serious, don't pick up that phone!

Know your story so you can rewrite it

It's imperative that you be completely honest with yourself as we progress with writing your current love story, i.e. the narrative you've crafted that's impacting the way you show up for love, what you expect from love and, possibly, why lasting love has escaped you until this moment in time. I ask that you approach this exercise without judgement or expectation of yourself or others. Your current love story is nobody's fault, and we can't change the past, but we can bring self-awareness to the present and craft a new, more rewarding story from now on.

Exercise 11

THE STORY THAT'S KEEPING YOU STUCK!

Now that we've identified all of the main components that make up your love story, I want you to sit down and actually write it. There are no rules. It can be as long or short as you like. You can write it as a list or a creative writing piece. I mean, if you're really in the mood you can write it in essay format (jokes, don't do that). But remember, this is the story you're currently running – the story that is most probably keeping you stuck. Nobody is going to be reading it, nobody is going to be judging you, you're just going to get wonderful clarity and self-awareness so that you can create a new, self-fulfilling love story moving forward.

I remember, clear as day, the first time I saw my old love story written down. Finally, I could see why my relationships all followed the same patterns, why I always attracted the same type of men and why I continued to make the same mistakes over and over (and over) again. Once you can see it for what it is – a story built on the past and a bunch of scripted fantasy – it's easy to change the narrative to a more rewarding and advantageous one. It all starts by deciding how you want to feel and adding those emotions to your personal vibration. From this point, you can move forward with a new love story and create the vibrational frequency that attracts the kind of love you deserve and are oh so worthy of.

Healing those love wounds

I wasn't about to let you dredge up all your childhood and past relationship guff and then leave you to marinate in it. So let's learn the lessons, forgive, heal and create a new love story, shall we? Because here's the craziest and most reassuring thing about old stories: once you heal them, you stop attracting them! Manifestation works both ways, my friend. So how about we get to manifesting that higher love and leave those past low vibrations exactly where they belong: in the past.

These next few exercises might take you a little to work through, depending on how much healing there is to be done. Take as much time as you need. No rush. You're going to write a series of letters. Under no circumstances are these letters to be sent. The magic is in the writing of them, not in the sending or receiving of them. I repeat DO NOT send these letters!

Exercise 12

TO ALL THE BOYS (OR GIRLS)
I'VE LOVED BEFORE

Okay, so depending on your dating history and your ability to find closure in relationships, this might take you a little longer. You're going to write a letter to each person you listed in the previous exercise that you're still affected by. I wrote eight letters!

Let them know why you still feel the way you do, why it triggers you, and the role they played in it. If there is anything you wish to say to them that you were never able to say to their face, pop it in this letter. This is your chance to get everything off your chest and I mean everything, because once this letter is complete, that's it – you're done with them, and no longer need to carry around the baggage you've been towing since you dated them. Also be conscious of the role that you played in the relationship. Perhaps there were things you did that you weren't proud of. This is your opportunity to apologise and make peace.

One more time, for the people at the back – DO NOT SEND THESE LETTERS!

The power of forgiveness

In both letter-writing exercises, I lovingly encouraged you to forgive each letter's recipient. It's an important step in the process of healing and finding closure. To forgive someone does not mean that you condone their behaviour, but rather that you choose to no longer hold it against them or begrudge them for past indiscretions. When we forgive, we're able to release the energy that was once so charged and allow it to be directed in a more loving and beneficial way. It's also important to be able to forgive yourself. It would be naïve to think that relationships are one-sided and that you don't have things that you are sorry for. While you might not be able to get the forgiveness you long for from the other person, you do always have the opportunity to forgive yourself. Often, when you leave a relationship, you hold on to unresolved guilt that feels like it could just eat you up and swallow you whole. The silver lining of guilt is that it's usually attached to a compromised value or belief – either yours or someone else's. By simply feeling that guilt, we're aware that a wrong has taken place. This kind of self-awareness has already kickstarted the healing process.

So, for extra points, if you feel there is a letter that needs to be written to you asking for forgiveness, then by all means, write it. Simply penning the words will begin the healing. If you're one of those high achievers and straight-A students, you might even like to read it aloud to yourself while looking in the mirror. POWERFUL STUFF.

Wondering what to do with all those letters?

It's a really personal experience, but once you've done the work of writing those feelings out and working through them, I believe the best thing you can do with those letters you've written is release yourself from them, energetically. Keeping them in box and reading over them again and again might seem cathartic at first, but ultimately that's just going to keep you stuck in the story.

I suggest releasing yourself from the energy of these letters by disposing of them in a way that feels empowering for you.

♥ **Burn them.** I like to go full mystic and burn them under a full moon (such a great time to release and let go). I tear the letters up into small pieces, throw them into a fire pit or fireplace and allow them to burn to ashes. You must have the intention to release the story along with the words you write down.

♥ **Bury them.** Tear them into small pieces and allow them to decompose in the dirt. I did this once and buried those pieces with some tomato seeds. I grew a beautiful tomato vine in place of the relationship I was releasing, and it felt good to see something grow in the place of a relationship that had died.

♥ **Put them on ice.** When I was a child, Mum didn't want me playing with fire or digging around ferociously in the dirt so she said I could write down anything that made me sad or angry, tear it into pieces, then pop it in an envelope and put that at the back of the freezer. I don't know how effective this actually is, but it felt good at the time.

- Chapter 7 -

Developing your personal love vibration

Let's get you a new lover, shall we? But first, let's work out what you're looking to bring out in yourself, in love. I believe a massive part of what we're all striving for when choosing and longing for a lover is to awaken to a part of ourselves we're convinced can't be accessed when we're alone. We're searching for the parts of us that light up when we're in love, and for emotions we're longing to feel that we've reserved for feeling when we're in union with another. We crave experiences that we've convinced ourselves need to be shared in order to be enjoyed.

I spoke of the pure essence of love in chapter 5 and explained how we've layered it in stories and romantic ideals, so let's uncover what love in its purest state looks like for you. It will be different for everybody, but remember these five things:

1. Pure love is unconditional. Not in the sense that it's fixed, but rather that it cannot be confined or defined by conditions placed on it.

2. Pure love is a state of being rather than doing or acting or receiving.

3. Pure love is how we relate to the world, not how the world relates to us. Love is not a means of validation or acceptance.

4. Pure love is not an extreme but a wholeness. Remember, the Law of Polarity states that a whole is made up of two opposites that complement each other. In the same way, love is the complete energy – not one of the extremes.

5. You already *are* pure love.

Exercise 13

FINDING YOUR PURE ESSENCE OF LOVE

Find a comfortable space to do this next exercise. I mean comfortable in the physical sense, but also comfortable for your emotions. Ideally, you'll feel safe, relaxed and perhaps even inspired in this space. Ensure you're free from distraction. You might like to light a candle, or burn some incense or essential oils. You could run also a bath, play some music, whatever you need to fully relax and connect to self. When I did this exercise, I put on some bright lipstick just to make myself feel super spesh, but these things are all adornments – they are absolutely not mandatory.

Step 1   Once you're comfortable, close your eyes.
Bring your awareness to your natural breath.
Note how you feel in your body.

Step 2   Take five deep belly breaths, allowing yourself
to relax just a little bit more on each exhale.

Step 3   Bring your awareness to your heart space.

Step 4   Allow yourself another five deep breaths,
this time allowing your heart to expand on each
inhale and soften on each exhale.

Step 5   Bring your awareness to the pure essence
of love that resides inside you. Feel this
pure essence of love in every cell of your body.
Allow it to wash over you.

Step 6   Observe the feelings that surface for you
at this time. No judgement, no critiques.
Just observe.

Open your eyes and write down the feelings that you felt when you tapped into the pure essence of love. When I did this exercise, I felt freedom, safety, joy, and a sense of expansiveness and fullness. Your feelings might be very different from mine. There is no right or wrong. But you're going to use these feelings from now on and add them to your personal vibration. Once you're aware how the pure essence of love feels for you, you have a benchmark by which to measure it going forward.

Exercise 14

GET CLEAR ON YOUR VALUES

We uncovered your core values in chapter 2 and decided that they were a good indicator of your personal vibration because when you're in alignment with them, you feel strong and when they're compromised you feel weak. Perhaps some of your core values were in relation to love, perhaps they weren't. Either way, let's focus now on those core values that you can attribute to love and relationships.

(MANIFESTION REMINDER: We're focusing on you and your role, not the values you're seeking in someone else. However, by staying true to your values and making them an integral piece of your personal vibration you're naturally attracting similar values towards you. Bonus!)

What are your core personal values when it comes to relationships? Remember, core values are best felt as feelings. You listed the feelings you attribute to the pure essence of love earlier in this chapter; perhaps some of these feelings can be included here. How do you want to feel in love?

My personal core love values are independence, freedom, security, playfulness and joy.

List lovers rejoice!

In chapter 6 of this book, I mentioned the list of traits that people often write to call in a new lover. And while this works for a small percentage of folks, I find, more often than not, a list like this can trip you up and leave you flat on your face.

That said, I'm still going to ask you to write a list, and it will be with the intention of calling in a new lover, but the focus is going to be 100 per cent on you and love, not you and the traits, qualities, aesthetic or profession of another person.

I will NOT compromise on my core love values when it comes to relationships. If I can't access these feelings that are an innate part of me, it's a good indication that I'm not in energetic alignment with the person I'm contemplating loving. Let me be very clear here, I'm not saying the other person needs to make me feel independent, free, secure, playful and joyful. No! What I'm saying is that those feelings are an innate part of me and what I value in love. If I can't continue to feel them and access them when I'm in a relationship or dating scenario, then it's a big red flag. Ya feel me?

When reflecting on my own dating history, it became apparent to me that I was constantly ignoring and dismissing red flags. My friends would often tell me I was too picky or too hard on others, and sometimes too hard on myself. So even though I saw the red flags, I chose to paint them white and fly them in surrender, along with all of the values I didn't even know I had. Don't do this.

I didn't write this book to tell you to love yourself more (although it never hurts to), or not to get super picky about what type of people you let into your life (although I give you permission to be as picky as you damn well like). I wrote it to help you tap in to your own unique frequency because that will work as your guide by highlighting what elevates you and what compromises your values, energy and integrity. This way, when red flags start popping up, you can recognise them immediately and make an informed choice about whether your personal vibration is worth compromising for this person.

How do you want to FEEL in love?

Let's take it a step further. Aside from your core values associated with love, how do you desire to *feel* in a relationship? Now, before you start listing off all of the ways you want your partner to make you feel, I want you to stop right there and take a deep breath.

Ask yourself two important, but seldom pondered questions:
Who do I want to be in a relationship?
and
How do I desire to feel in a relationship?

Remember when I told you about the ice-queen version of me who surfaced when I was with Kurt? Gross! I never want to be that person. I didn't like her at all. And remember when I told you about the way I felt in myself (not the way he made me feel) when I was with Jack? That's the vibrational frequency I desire. I really bloody liked myself in that relationship. I liked the person I was, how I showed up for me and for him, how confident I felt, and how I also felt smart, funny and sexy. I liked who I was with my friends, I enjoyed how I showed up to work, and I loved how I kept my independence while also sharing my life with someone else. I felt so strong, healthy, abundant, free, safe and worthy in my own right, and because of that, I happened to attract a man who made me feel those things, too.

Do you know how I did that? Because I was all those things long before Jack turned up on my doorstep (quite literally, but you'll hear that story later). And not only was I all of those things before I met him, but I was able to easily maintain them while in a relationship with him, and that is the end goal here, my friends.

Do you know yourself (warts and all)? Do you accept yourself (warts and all)? Can you be your authentic self all while dating and in a relationship with another? This is important, because if you can be your most authentic self in a cave on a mountain removed from civilisation, that is wonderful but completely useless (and some might say lonely). But if you can be yourself, radiate authenticity, and use that as a measure of whether or not someone is the right fit for you while getting to know one another, well, then it's a really strong way to build a relationship.

YOU are responsible for your own feelings. You are responsible for the qualities you bring into a relationship and in turn the qualities you attract in another person. You play a much bigger role in the dating experience than you give yourself credit for, and once you're hyper aware of who you are with a strong personal vibration, you honestly hold all of the power.

You'll know when to walk away (or run). Kenny Rogers knew! Sure, he may have been taking about gambling, but it totally applies to dating, too.

Remember Nick? I've dated a bunch of Nicks. And as much as I would like to say a strong vibration only attracts perfect matches, it's just not the case. But what it does do is become a foolproof vetting tool so that you don't waste your time on the Nicks and Kurts of this world.

Exercise 15

A LIST THAT ACTUALLY WORKS!

Let's scrap that tired old list of traits and professional aspirations your potential partner needs to have. Instead, it's time to write a new list, this time one that considers how you want to feel when you're in a relationship. If you feel the way you intend to feel in a relationship, does it really matter if he's not a boat-building, lasagna-cooking, wine-tasting astrophysicist?

Ask yourself what qualities you would like to radiate while in a relationship. (Psst, they'll also probably end up being the qualities you attract in another.) Let's add these to your personal vibration now. We can call them your love GPS if you like (I mean, why wouldn't you?). I'll start.

Independence, freedom and trust are so important to me in a relationship. So I ensure that I have an awareness of what independence and freedom feel like for me outside of a relationship and that I can trust myself and my own choices knowing I would expect the same thing from my partner. Independence, freedom and trust make up a big part of my personal vibration.

Kindness, generosity and compassion are such virtues, but there have been times in certain relationships where I've found it really hard to be those things. This is never okay. If I struggle to show kindness, generosity and compassion, I know I'm not in the right relationship.

These qualities are such an integral part of my personal vibration. If I'm unable to access them, I know something isn't right.

Fun, laughter and play are things I focus on more and more as I get older. If I'm not having fun and laughing, I know my vibration is off big time. I'm also aware that fun, laughter and play need to be part of who I am rather than what I can only feel when I'm with a partner, so I make sure to cultivate these qualities as part of what makes up my personal vibration on the reg.

Okay, now it's your turn.

Write down as many qualities as you'd like; my list certainly doesn't stop with the words above. What's most important here is that you're thinking of the ways *you* can make yourself feel, not the things you expect the other person to make you feel. If you take nothing else from this book, please let this one piece of advice sink in.

Time to rewrite your love story

You've figured out what your core values are when it comes to love, and how you desire to feel in love – and these two things will have added some serious juice to your personal vibration. From this space, you can write a new love story that allows you to approach love based on your own intrinsic qualities and principles rather than a story shaped by your past relationships, a childhood lens or the irritating yet oddly endearing characters played by the likes of Hugh Grant.

By staying aligned and vibrating on the frequency of your new story, you're not only creating an epic love GPS system but you're attracting the kind of love you deserve directly into your orbit. Before you get to your new love story (I know, I'm seriously drawing this thing out) I have one more exercise for you to do. I promise the waiting will be worth it.

Exercise 16

WHAT DOES LOVE FEEL LIKE?

If you remove the connection between the feeling of love and romantic relationships, what things in your life make you feel love? For me it's the sound of kids laughing uncontrollably, the feeling of summer rain on my skin, lying in savasana after a sweaty yoga class, diving into the ocean, lazy Sunday mornings (I'm partial to lazy Wednesday mornings, too), watching a movie on my own with an oversized bucket of popcorn, long phone chats with old friends or cooking while listening to my favourite tunes.

I could go on for pages, but you get the picture. Sometimes, removing the romantic connotations of love enables us to go back to that pure essence of love I've been banging on about throughout Part Two of this book.

Write down all of the things that make you feel love that are not associated with romantic relationships. These things will help you conjure up the feeling of love so that you can apply it to your new love story.

Exercise 17

FINALLY, THIS IS IT! YOUR NEW LOVE STORY

Now, with the lessons of the previous exercises fresh in your mind, can you craft your new love story and the way you perceive love based on your love values, how you want to feel in love and the way the essence of pure love makes you feel (romantic or otherwise)?

Use any one of these prompts to start you off:

Healthy love is ...

A strong and loving relationship is ...

I'll know that my love vibration has found its match when ...

Exercise 18

MANIFESTING YOUR NEW LOVE STORY

I want to bring your awareness back to the Manifestation Equation, which I introduced you to way back in chapter 1. Now that you've written your new love story, it's prime time to be applying the principles of manifestation to put you on the well-established path of creating a higher love.

>>

>>

Remember, the Manifestation Equation looks like this:

Thoughts + Feelings + Action + Faith = Manifestation

Ask yourself the following:

Thoughts: *Are my thoughts aligned with my new love story?* When you catch thoughts creeping in that support your old story, the one that kept you stuck and most likely single, see if you can switch your thought right in that moment to one that supports your new love story.

Feelings: *Are my feelings aligned with my love vibration?* You just wrote a really beautiful list of the types of feelings you want to radiate in a relationship. Writing them down isn't going to do much unless you take the time to actually feel them NOW. Don't wait until you're in a relationship to feel all those things, feel them in any way you can right this second because this is what is going to turn you into a love magnet.

Actions: *Are my actions aligned with the love I want to create?* In Part Three, I'm going to take you through some really practical steps to get you physically dating. This is the action piece, but what's important is that the actions you choose to take are in support of your new love story, not working against it. You must take responsibility for the actions you take in regard to your life, ensuring that they are aligned with the love you want to create. A great example of this would be sitting at home in your PJs night after night and wondering why you're still single. Or dating someone who makes you feel shit and dampens your vibration because you'd rather be with someone, anyone, than be alone.

Faith: *Do I trust that I'm capable of experiencing a higher love and that the universe is looking out for me?* If you're struggling with the faith piece, I urge you to revisit the exercises on your personal vibration. Most of the time, faith in yourself comes down to your level of self-worth, which we also discussed in chapter 1. You must believe that you're worthy and deserving of the new love story you've written for yourself, and the best way to do this is to keep working at strengthening your personal vibration.

If you can keep checking back in with each element of the Manifestation Equation and how it pertains to the new love story you've penned for yourself, you're going to be blown away by the impact it has on your love life.

Congratulations! You are officially a love magnet. A healthy, nourishing, authentic love magnet that will attract all sorts of weird, wonderful and questionable love, but that has an inbuilt radar attached (your personal vibration) that will filter out anything and anyone that is not in your highest interest and your quest for a 'higher love'.

Okay, let's do a quick recap of what you've learned in the so far because once we get to the next chapter, you're going to start dating. And until you master the teachings in the first two parts of this book, you'll likely struggle to get true value out of the steps contained in Part Three.

♥ You learned all about your personal vibration and why it's so important to be super clear when it's strong and when it's weak.

♥ You discovered that values, intuition and natural talents are all components of your personal vibration, and it's your responsibility to stay in alignment with the things that strengthen it.

♥ You learned about the things that can weaken your personal vibration, including social media, comparison, external validation, people-pleasing and energy vampires.

♥ You discovered the importance of setting healthy boundaries and how looking after your health affects your personal vibration big time.

♥ You took a look at some of the gaps in your life that you've been waiting for a partner to fill and decided to fill them yourself.

♥ You discovered that love has been misinterpreted, catastrophised and romanticised but it is actually a really simple and pure state of being.

♥ You learned that your love story that's been dictating your dating and relationships has been built on your experience with love growing up, Hollywood ideals and every crush, date, mate and pash you've likely ever had.

♥ You reinvented your love story by going back to the pure essence of love and adding it to your personal vibration, i.e. you made yourself into a love magnet!

You're now prepped and primed to attract a higher love.

PART THREE

DATING ... DIFFERENTLY

I wish I could tell you that this book has the power to prevent you from ever experiencing a bad date again. It doesn't. In fact, if you do what I ask, and date more, odds are a few of those dates will be with utter douchebags (they're tricky tricksters, you don't always see them coming). But I'm not here for the douchebags of the world, I'm here for *you*. To let you know that whether they're a frog, a prince, a fun time or a hard no, YOU are still a bright spark of joy who can be certain a bad date is just a bad date, and not a reflection of you.

You may have ended up here, with this book in your hands, for many different reasons. Maybe you're notoriously single or you've walked out on a long-term relationship. Perhaps you've just been dumped or perhaps you're dipping your toe back in the water after a long dry spell ... either way, the same principles apply. Dating is your opportunity to find love, but it's also a vetting process. So, if a higher love is what you're in the market for, your chances will increase exponentially if you're actively going on dates. Plus, that personal vibration you've worked so hard on in the first two parts of this book is about to become your dating armour. Not to keep you guarded, but to make you braver so that you take more chances (always advantageous when meeting new people) and, if you do come face to face with disappointment or heartbreak (it's the risk that comes with dating), brave enough to know you'll survive it.

This is where we really dive deep into the Action part of the Manifestation Equation I introduced you to way back in chapter 1. The Law of Action states that *you must do the things and perform the actions necessary to achieve what you are setting out to do.* In this case the action is dating, and you're going to be actively doing it, not just thinking about it. So please approach this part of the book with an open mind and a can-do attitude. Take what resonates, leave what doesn't, but know that not only do I have your back, I've also done a lot of the legwork for you so you don't have to waste your time making some of the mistakes that I did. (You're welcome.)

Chapter 8

Dating ain't what it used to be

I don't know how old you are. It doesn't matter much. You could be 21 or 61, the fact is if you're currently single and looking to date, you are dating in THIS time in history and it is somewhat different from the dating that took place in the decades and centuries before now. Or is it?

The world progresses not just as the generations shift but also as trends come and go – fashion, literary, culinary or otherwise. Technology advances, chivalry dies and is then resurrected with conditions, caveats and clauses to protect and empower while also confusing and blurring lines in the process. Engaging conversation is labelled 'banter', whether you're a dog or cat person holds significant weight, as does your affinity to 'Netflix and chill'. Suddenly, acronyms like INFJ and ENTP are letters that weigh heavily on your future romances as you search for hours on end through what is essentially a catalogue of potential suitors while sporting sweats, greasy locks and corn-chip-coated fingers.

In a recent, somewhat tipsy, conversation at the pub, I cornered a table of men in their early thirties who had just finished work, after I'd witnessed one of them flicking through a dating app while sitting in a venue full of (one would assume) available women. I asked them when they last picked up a woman in the wild (aka the pub). Two of them were married and opted out of my interrogation, the other three laughed and said it had been a few years. 'WHY?' I asked with perhaps too much gusto. 'I guess it's just easier to pick them up on an app. Less rejection, less hassle, no commitment. Why do you ask? Are you single?' I gave them my rehearsed spiel about writing a book about dating, at which point they all began to fidget uncomfortably in their seats (common reaction) before crying in unison, 'Please help us!'

Well, professional men in your early thirties, you can relax; you're not doing anything wrong – well, at least most of you aren't. It's the reality of dating these days. We women are progressively (or perhaps less progressively) moving away from flirtatious lash batting at the bar, and into flirtatious and non-committal banter across our smartphones. If you ask women, collectively, they're not too stoked about it, and if you ask men, it seems they, too, long for the courting customs of yesteryear, although they do prefer being shielded from rejection, and can you blame them?

This shift in dating happened in what may feel like an overnight type of fashion, but really it's been slowly shifting as the internet and social media have taken over our very existence. We can book flights, transfer money, track our heart rates, sleep patterns, menstrual cycles and fertility, order food straight to our front door from the fine-dining restaurant a few suburbs away, meditate, apply for a house rental, interview for a job and even become an ordained celebrant right from our devices. Why not use them to find a soulmate, too?

It all (officially) began in 1995 when the first online dating site, Match.com, launched in America, but the practice of looking for love via posting in public forums dates as far back as 1695, when people started placing ads in newspapers looking for their one true love.

How personal ads turned into digital dating

1695
The first personal ad is placed in a British newspaper. These ads are usually last-ditch attempts by single men who are getting too old for bachelorhood. (If only men had the same standards now. #peterpansyndrome)

1800s
Personal ads in newspapers get a little saucy when aristocrats use them to engage in scandalous romantic entanglements (think Tinder meets Ashley Madison). This is also around the time that dating scams became a thing, with con-artists targeting vulnerable wealthy single women (*Dirty John*, anyone?).

1959
Computerised matchmaking is born when a couple of Stanford University students conduct a project called 'Happy Families Planning Service' (not quite as catchy as Tinder). Using an IBM

650 computer and punch-card questionnaires, the students paired 49 men with 49 women.

1965

Operation Match launches when uni students Jeff Tarr and Vaughan Morrill conduct a social experiment using an IBM 1401 and a questionnaire. Six months after the launch, some 90,000 Operation Match questionnaires had been received. In the late 1960s, two more computer and questionnaire dating services emerged: Eros in 1965 and Data-Mate in 1968.

1960s–70s

The Dating Game – where singles interview and choose partners in front of a live audience – airs on US TV and becomes a hit.

1980s

Daters start to connect digitally on electronic bulletin boards and chat rooms. This is also the decade when dating hits mainstream pop culture thanks to more dating television shows such as the UK's *Blind Date* (*Perfect Match* in Australia).

1995

Match.com, the first online dating site, launches followed by Jdate in 1997, the first online dating site targeted at single Jewish women and men.

1998

The movie *You've Got Mail* with Meg Ryan and Tom Hanks hits cinemas and normalises the idea of finding love online.

2002

The very first season of reality dating show *The Bachelor* launches in America.

Early 2000s

Various dating apps launch but none rival the successes of Grindr in 2009 and Tinder in 2012.

2009

Grindr launches the first location-based dating app geared towards LGBTQ users.

2012

Tinder launches, completely changing the way people hook up. The intention behind it was to create a social platform where users could meet people they didn't know or wouldn't usually meet. Tinder patented its swiping option, and the phrases 'swipe right' and 'swipe left' swiftly become part of our everyday dating vernacular.

2014

Bumble launches its location-based dating app in which matches are made but conversation can only be initiated by women.

There are hundreds of other matching sites, dating apps and television shows that could be included on this timeline. The point of giving you this walk down Cupid's memory lane is to illustrate that the dating services available today aren't a completely new phenomenon, even though at times it can still feel new and scary (just me?).

If there's one thing that timeline shows, it's that people have been dating 'unconventionally' and in many forms since the 1600s. I'd go so far as to say that 300+ years of unconventional dating makes it kind of conventional. So if you're one of those people who are *still* resisting digital dating, it might be time to change your tune. We'll talk a lot about dating online and via apps over the next few chapters, and sometimes I'll speak favourably about it – interweaving successful online dating stories of my own with those from other people. Other times, I'll wrap my frustration up in a funny anecdote or a disastrous tale. But what I want you to know right here, right now, is that although dating has changed considerably, as most things do through shifting decades, it's also changed very little in the ways that matter. Women's rights and increasing economic agency, changing governments, social climates and upgraded technology have altered the dating landscape, but not completely. Some 'old-fashioned' modes of courting may be gone, but they're not forgotten. They still exist even in the realms of online dating. And while it feels like the 'rules' have changed (mostly because many of them were shit and deserved a makeover), many of the same principles still apply. We'll be looking at some dating *suggestions* – ones better suited to you and your particular personal vibration.

It's still 100 per cent possible to meet someone away from your device, and we'll explore some of those ways in the next chapter. That said, I would like you to be at least open to the idea of dating online. Banish the stigma of catfishing horror stories and instant hook-ups because, truth be told, you can be just as fooled by someone IRL as you can be across the safety of your device.

Have the goal posts of love moved?

It's easy to fall into the trap of thinking that our definition of happily ever after hasn't shifted since our grandparents' generation, but the truth is a bunch of changes have heavily impacted our relationship goals for the better, and they're worth noting if you're still trying to replicate the simplicity of the love Grandma and Grandpa had for each other.

If finding a love match now feels harder than you imagine it would have been for past generations, consider that our expectations have shifted monumentally. Seventy-odd years ago, marriage was a partnership based on social status, companionship and financial stability. Love, passion and attraction weren't high on either a man's nor a woman's priority list. Now, we expect our partner to be our best friend, lover, entertainer, fixer, doer, baker and candlestick maker. Is this any better? Personally, I've never been in the market for a candlestick maker, though I'm not above finding one. However, I do believe that the added pressure we now place on ourselves to find the 'perfect' partner (or at least what we believe perfection to be) means that we're most likely missing out on a bunch of above-adequate partners who would make us blissfully happy.

When trying to wrap your head around why finding a partner feels so much tricker these days then in previous generations, a few other factors need to be considered . . .

We're getting married older. According to the Australian Bureau of Statistics, in 2018 the average age at marriage was 32.4 years for men and 30.5 years for women; in 1984 the average age was 27 for men and 24 for women; and in 1966 the average age was 26 for men and 22 for women. What changed? Well, higher education has become a priority for school leavers as has a flourishing career. Women especially are wanting to have a career before getting married and starting a family.

Women are financially independent. Women are more likely to seek financial independence from their partner, (thanks to those career aspirations I just mentioned) and don't marry necessarily for the security of a working husband.

We want to see the world. Travel (at least pre-pandemic) is a lot more affordable and attainable for young people, and we're making the most of it in our twenties before settling down.

We talk, express and communicate more. This has increased considerably over the last few decades, with couples encouraging more open and transparent communication. As a result, communication compatibility has become one of the things we prioritise when searching for an ideal partner.

Gender roles are evolving. I'm not going to profess this has changed across the board but there's definitely been a shift in acceptance of men staying home while women go to work. We've seen a significant increase in shared responsibility for household duties, childcare and expenses.

Diversity is more accepted. We have the freedom to marry outside our religion, ethnicity and cultural background, where previously this was rare. We also have the freedom (in many countries, anyway) to marry people of the same sex or, of course, not marry at all.

As we forge ahead with the practicalities of dating, I want to assure you that, although the landscape in which we date has most definitely shifted, the way we connect, communicate and form an attraction is essentially the same. If you can focus on walking into the dating experience sure of who you are and what you value and desire, and with an awareness of what your personal vibration feels like when it's strong, then you're leagues above most other fish in the sea.

- Chapter 9 -

How to land a hot date

This is what you're here for, right? To land a hot date. To find out the secret sauce recipe. Well, I have good news and I have great news. The good news is that I have most of the ingredients for you to make a fabulously delicious sauce that you're going to love pouring all over yourself (too far with the sauce analogy? Sorry!). The great news is that the secret ingredient is you!

So while there's no big reveal in this chapter that you likely don't already know, there are a bunch of super helpful and practical tips to get you dating. And when I say dating, what I mean is going out on physical dates. It's crazy how many people say they're dating, yet haven't been on an actual date for many, many months (or years).

If this is you (it was me for three years) you're in the right place. You got through the first two parts of this book, which likely revealed a few *whoa* and *aha* moments about your dating/ love life up until now, and you're in a better position than ever before to be on the prowl for a new lover, summer fling or life partner.

If you've been scarred by the 'dating scene' in the past, know that you're done with that. You've officially left it behind in your old love story. The new love story you've written hopefully has filled you with the impetus to get back out there with a fresh slate, a strong personal vibration and clarity about how you want your next relationship to feel.

But before we progress, know this: the dating scene is a construct. It was fabricated by women's' mags, dating sites and movies. There is no 'scene', there are just people (like you and me) dating other people (again, like you and me) in the hope of meeting someone to form a connection with. The word 'scene' used to trip me up, like I was joining a sorority of desperate singles all vying for a limited number of potential suitors. It's not like that at all. Think of dating as an opportunity to take your personal vibration out in the world and rub against other vibrations to see if there's a match for your frequency. Note that no actual physical rubbing up against is required (unless you're ready and there's consent and, well, I'll leave the hanky-panky, extracurricular activities to your discretion).

Before I dish out some super helpful information that you're going to treasure forever and ever, please promise yourself one thing: you WILL date. Reading about dating is not dating. Sitting on your couch in your sweats thinking about dating is not dating. Living vicariously through the dates your friends go on is not dating. And finally, watching *The Bachelor* and choosing the winner in the first episode and then investing in their happy ending is definitely not dating. Are we clear?

Where do you even meet people these days?

In da club? At a poetry reading? At your friend's birthday barbecue? On a dating app? Look, I can't comment on da club – it's been a while – but I can say a definitive yes to all of the above. When it comes to dating, you can split the ways you meet people into three categories.

1. **Organically.** By this I mean out in public: e.g. at a bar, at the bus stop, in a bookshop or in a number of other places that start with B and some that don't.

2. **A set-up.** This is when your mates, family or work colleagues decide that they have the perfect match for you and organise a hook-up. Sometimes it's a blind date, sometimes you already know each other, sometimes it's sprung on you when you least expect it.

3. **Digital dating.** Yes, I'm talking apps, dating sites and the various matchmaking services we covered in the last chapter.

But here's the thing: all of the above are just means to an end. Whether you meet someone organically, through a set-up or by swiping right, you still have to go on a date with them. So while 'organic' might feel more predestined, is it really any different from the set-ups or digital dating? I'm here to controversially say NO. And here's a really unsexy, yet great hypothetical scenario that proves my point.

Let's say you're in the market for a new job. You have the following three options:

a) Sit in a café or bar and wait for your dream job to come to you. Sometimes, dream jobs do seemingly land in your lap, but you could be waiting a long time, and in the meantime you're unemployed.

b) Hop on a computer and browse a job site for advertised jobs, then apply for the ones best suited to you and wait for a response. This is the most efficient of the three methods, and it gives you the best chance of at least getting an interview.

c) Ask friends, family and colleagues if they have any connections or know of any available jobs in your industry. This feels a little safer. They can provide you with a glowing reference, so you feel like you've got a leg-up on other candidates. But your success does rest on someone knowing someone and the perfect job just waiting in the wings.

Option A seems like the least proactive and most unlikely way to land a job, yet when it comes to dating it's the path we convince ourselves is the most ... romantic? Kismet? Effortless? ... Stupid!

I'm torn here – torn about what advice is going to serve you best. On the one hand, I've spent the first half of this book turning you into a vibrating love magnet (I know that sounds like a sex toy, but it's definitely not a sex toy). You are now primed to attract people and experiences that are energetically aligned with the frequency of your vibration. And yeah, this will likely mean that you run into them in the freezer section of your local supermarket, or that you happen to pull your mats out beside each other at your next yoga class. These encounters are more likely to occur when you're vibrating on your own authentic frequency, and I hope this brings you comfort, I really do. But this information and new superpower mustn't make you lazy. It doesn't matter how strong your personal vibration is if you're only vibrating in the confines of your own house or the places you always frequent and the same coupled-up social circles you always spend time in.

Rather, because of this superhero-level vibration you've just built for yourself, I want you to be braver. Put yourself out there knowing that you have an inbuilt radar that will help you sort through what is and isn't in your highest interest; it will give you a much greater chance of meeting people who you're in alignment with. And yes, some of those people can be found on a dating app (I'll tell you lots of beautiful stories to prove this point soon enough).

Take risks. Date a few frogs. Enjoy the experience. Because if there's one thing that I want you to take away from this book, it's that dating is so much more fun when you're walking in as a whole person who is clear on their values, what excites them and what they're not willing to compromise on. So you meet a few duds, so what! Do you know what's sexier than finding the perfect partner? Being a completely whole person who can walk away if it doesn't work out and be fine. With this in mind, let's have a look at the various ways you can meet people and land yourself a hot date.

App(ropriate) behaviour

I've professed countless times to countless people that dating apps are shit. When you choose people based on their energy and how their vibration aligns with yours – as I like to do – dating apps become a bit of a barrier. I would rant to anyone who would listen, 'You can't read someone's energy through an app,' but now I think that was an excuse I was using to explain why I wasn't using an app. The real reason was that I just wasn't comfortable with the idea of not being able to woo a man in the flesh with my titillating hip-sways, the dulcet tones of my radio voice, my compassionate arm-touches, my hair swept to the side or my flirtatious and interested giggle. 'OMG, you are *so* funny.'

The most common complaints I hear about dating apps are:

- ♥ 'They're SO superficial.'
- ♥ 'You don't know who the person is.'
- ♥ 'They're sleazy.'
- ♥ 'It feels forced.'
- ♥ 'It feels desperate.'

I'm sure you've got your own list of complaints, and every single one of these is legitimate, for sure. But these complaints are also true for any other form of dating. When you see someone across the bar, the party, or the travel section of your quaint local bookstore, your initial impression is based on aesthetics. Sure, they might be reading a book about the Seychelles that piques your interest or sporting a jumper you like. Perhaps it's the swagger of their step or the sensual sounds of their speech, but without truly knowing a person or having an opportunity to get to the crux of who they are, all we have to go on, initially, is information that can only be classified as superficial.

As for dating via apps feeling 'forced', 'desperate' and 'sleazy'? Totally! But I've also been fooled by many a handsome man disguising his sleazy ways behind things far less incriminating than a wholesome profile pic and a generous, well-written bio. I've also most certainly initiated a date with an 'accidental' stumble, a well-placed drink order or by boldly striking up a conversation. At times in my life, I'm sure I've entered a party or venue with desperation seeping from my pores. These are all symptoms of dating and they're not reserved for the digital dating experience. So let's not treat digital dating as 'other'; let's see it for what it is: a handy tool for lining up real-life dates. Because it's THE easiest, most foolproof way to date – physically, in the flesh, in real time, right now!

As demonstrated in the previous chapter, the old-fashioned bar pick-up isn't the way men prowl anymore (or women, for that matter). Yes, we've got lazy. Yes, it's not a good excuse. And no, no one is particularly happy about it, but it's a reality and honestly, I think there are ways of tackling dating on an app that you'll really enjoy.

The pros and cons of dating apps

Let's put all our cards on the table from the get-go. I feel like you've got a hefty list of cons, so let's start by addressing some of those and then I'll see your cons and raise you a few pros that might just get you on board.

Cons

♥ There are people out there who will be very different in
the flesh from who they portray in their profile, but again,
this is also true for people you meet out in the real world.
In one way or another, we're all putting our best foot
forward when it comes to first impressions. And yeah,
sometimes someone's best foot is not the real them.

♥ It's tricky to read someone's energy through an app.
Although there have been instances where I've got
a read on someone's energy through their online profile,
more often than not, it's tricky to tell if someone is
a vibrational match through your device.

♥ It can feel superficial. We covered this earlier, but it
bears repeating because I'm in full agreement that it
can feel that way. I hate that when I swipe, I'm swiping
mostly based on how photogenic a person is. Sure, their
profile can make me curious, but not if their photo
doesn't catch my eye first. Of the eight men I've been
in a relationship with I honestly think I would have only
swiped for three of them. Two of them I actually met on
an app, and if I'm being honest, the only reason I swiped
for them was because their bios either made me laugh
or intrigued me; it wasn't because I thought they were
my type or particularly handsome.

♥ It takes the romance out of it. Yes, initially it absolutely
does. But I have definitely had romantic sparks fly on
first dates set up through a dating app. In fact, I've had
romance build through the initial back-and-forth chat
that's still happening within the app.

Pros

♥ Apps are a fast and efficient way to set up a date.

♥ You can pick and choose who you give your time to by having a non-committal text conversation before deciding to meet in the flesh.

♥ You can be quite direct with your questions straight away. This is accepted and encouraged.

♥ A well-put-together profile will tell you up front their intention for being on the app. You'll know whether they are looking for a relationship or just something casual, and it's also a great way to avoid Scorpios. (Jokes.)

♥ Apps are an excellent way to dip your toe back in the dating pool.

♥ You can talk to a few different people at once and only move forward with the people you genuinely feel a connection with.

Setting up a magnetic profile

As a writer, I have an unfair advantage when it comes to writing online dating bios. I insert tone, wit and lyrical timing that encapsulates my personality and quirks in one paragraph. It's lost on most, but the fish (I mean men) it does hook are already starting to vibe with who I am (that's if they read it; most men don't, FYI). I'm also guilty of penning bios for many a friend, because, let's be honest, a sea of emojis may seem like a clever idea but it's lazy and predictable, plus it wastes an opportunity to put your best foot forward by providing a literary snapshot of your vibration. I enjoy doing this and I feel like I'm doing my friends a favour, but I really should stop. I'm actually doing them – as well as the men and women they're trying to pick up – a massive disservice. If you're serious about finding a partner on an app you MUST show up 100 per cent, and this includes writing a bio (yourself) and sharing as much of your authentic self as you can in it.

Perhaps I judge profile bios more harshly than I should. But for me, a grammatically correct, humorous, intelligent bio is integral to my decision to swipe left or right. I feel I can connect and understand more about a person through their use of the English language than through their choice of selfie. But it also shows effort, intention and integrity, and by including a bio they're asking me to evaluate them on more than just their chiselled abs and shiny motorcycle.

This applies in reverse, too. The bio you choose to share is your chance to take your personal vibration out for a spin. Can you describe yourself in a way that gives potential suitors a snapshot of your true character? This is a great opportunity to sell yourself beyond your physical attributes. When drafting yours, here are some things you might like to consider:

♥ What sets you apart from every other person on the app? Think of a few things, and then include them. You don't want to get lost in a sea of faces and boring bios.

♥ Inject your sense of humour. Only do this if your sense of humour is a trait you wish to display; if you find it tricky to be funny, don't force it. Also, if a joke needs to be explained, it's not the kind of joke that's appropriate for an app bio – trust me!

♥ Be honest. This doesn't mean putting all your cards on the table, but don't lie or say things you think potential partners want to hear. A girlfriend of mine decided it would be appealing to say she enjoyed whisky, which seems super harmless, but every time she went on a date, the guy would order her a whisky on the rocks and she'd have to sit there forcing down a spirit she despised.

♥ Don't be afraid to be up front about why you're on a dating app. What are you interested in finding? Are you looking for something casual?

♥ Avoid self-deprecation. I get that it can be funny, and I'm definitely guilty of using it, but save it for your witty face-to-face banter (which will give it context). Putting yourself down as an opening gambit is confusing and detrimental – it also might attract a downright creep. Don't do it.

A picture is worth a thousand words

I spoke to both men and women to ask what they look for in dating app profile pictures. They had lots to say. I'll share their feedback with you first, and then let's talk about your profile pics. Both sexes had the following things to share:

NO FILTERS! This was yelled at me by everyone I surveyed. YELLED! And I can understand why. Filters are not an accurate representation of you – especially if they include dog ears and cartoon eyes. Until they invent a way for you to look like a filter in the real world, STOP! No more!

Ensure your photos are recent. Within the last 24 months is fair, but within the year is even better. If your intention is to get off the apps and actually have a relationship with someone, there's going to come a point when they meet the real you. You need to look like the person in the photos.

Aesthetic changes need to be documented. If you have changed your hair colour, had collagen, botox, or any other cosmetic treatment, tattooed your eyebrows, shaved your beard (fellas, I'm looking at you) or had your boobs/nose/chin done, zero judgement, but make sure your photos look like the you who's going to rock up to your first date. And I know this is a sensitive subject, but this also applies to weight gain and loss. If you've gained a few kilos since the pics you've posted, it's okay. But it's important that the person you're portraying is you. It's important for your personal vibration that you're fully aligned with what you are presenting to the other person. When you meet someone on the street, they're meeting the real-life version of you. Dating apps shouldn't be any different.

Full-body shots! Okay so when EVERYONE said this to me, I got defensive. I stood up for me, for you, for everyone who is a little self-conscious about their body (which, honestly, I think is most people). But the consensus was the same. It's not that you're being judged on your body, it's just an accurate portrayal of the person they'll be meeting on this date. And that's only fair, right? Ask yourself why you're hiding your banging bod. They're bound to meet more than just your head eventually.

Women were particularly vocal about profile pics

And they said …

'Dudes, stop posting photos of yourself surrounded by a bunch of drunk women in short skirts!' – No woman finds this attractive.

They also said:

'Nobody finds beer bongs endearing.' – I tend to agree.

'Gym selfies impress nobody!' – I concur.

And on the subject of selfies …

'WHY ARE YOU HOLDING THE CAMERA SO GODDAMN CLOSE TO YOUR FACE?' – Nobody wants to see up your nostrils, mate! It's weird and creepy.

'Stop posting pics of your car, truck, motorcycle that you're not in! Are you a transformer?' – LOL!

'Make sure you post pics of you on your own. When you're in a group we have no idea who the F you are!' – I've actually turned up to a date thinking I was meeting the 'other guy' in his pics. (#awkward)

'Take off your sunglasses.' – No seriously, remove them, we want to see into your soul!

'Put your shirt back on! If we can't post topless pics, neither can you!' (#equality)

'Do not post a photo of you with your ex.' – And if it's your sister, cousin or best friend, tell us!

'If you have a dog, include it in your pics PLEASE.'
– I mean, it's just rude not to.

But …

'Don't use other people's babies to make yourself appear paternal!'
– Creepy.

(Wow, we really are demanding, aren't we?)

And the men said …

'No duck faces' and *'NO FILTERS'*. – They feel very strongly about the filter thing!

That's pretty much all they said. It seems they're less fussed about how women pose for photos.

Some extra tips from me to you

- ♥ **Limit the selfies.** One or two is fine but try to mix them up with pics taken of you having fun. I hate posing for photos, so I actually have very few pics that aren't professional photos or selfies. This makes me look like I have no friends. Which isn't true! If you don't have any photos, ask a friend or family member to take one.
- ♥ **Do include a full-body pic.** You don't have to be in your activewear or bikini, but, energetically, I believe it's important to show up on the app. Hiding yourself doesn't benefit you or them.
- ♥ **Choose pics that illustrate your personality.** If you like to travel, include some travel shots; if you're into bird watching, hiking, fishing or papier-mâché, include pics

that demonstrate this. Just make sure you're visible in the pic. A shot of the Eiffel Tower and you as a tiny spec is helpful to no one other than a Francophile.

❤ **Always smile – naturally.** Reserve those blue-steel, duck faces, pouts or deep-in-thought shots for Instagram.

❤ **Take off your sunglasses, ski mask, hat and hoodie.** In other words, pretend you're at immigration. We need to make a positive ID.

Tips for swiping

It took some time for me to get on the apps. I was convinced they were superficial, so when I finally succumbed, I vowed to distribute my swipes fairly. I told myself, *Thou shalt not judge them by their lack of good lighting, inability to take a decent selfie or poor choice of footwear*, but before I knew it, I'd spent a half hour I'd never get back swiping left (that means no way, no how) on a bunch of men I knew nothing about. And here we run into a common dating app double standard: please do not judgeth me on my pictures, but I will most certainly judgeth you.

As time went on, I loosened up a little. I threw men with poor bios a rightward swipe if they could take a decent picture. I'd also dish out a few right flicks if their bio made me giggle, left me wanting to know more or displayed decent sentence structure (desperate times) – even if their pics were more 'serial killer' than 'take home to Mum and Dad'. And this is when dating on apps got good. Because you know what? Sometimes great humans are just shit at writing nice things about themselves and taking decent photos.

All dating apps differ slightly in their functionality, but they share the same basic premise, which is this: when you both say 'yes' to each other by either swiping right, or 'liking', or some other confirmation of, 'Yeah, I see potential in you,' then a match has been made and communication can commence. This is no different from when your eyes meet across the bar, or when a friend introduces you, or you strike up conversation in your local coffee shop. There's still that first moment where you both energetically agree to 'see where this goes'.

It's very easy to get stuck in the superficiality of 'the swipe'. I urge you to be open to the people who you are tempted to sweep to the left. Read their bio. Feel into their energy. Try not to make judgements based on their star sign. The same goes for those you swipe right on. But if you're looking for a relationship and they've clearly stated they're after something casual, don't swipe. Same applies if they don't want kids and you do, or if they're a party animal and you're three years sober. Your challenge, should you choose to accept it, is to swipe right for somebody you wouldn't ordinarily swipe for because of their sunglasses or profession or something equally superficial and really not a make or break. What's the worst that can happen? A match doesn't lock you in to anything ... Give it a go.

It's completely normal to get excited when you get a match, but even then, a match doesn't mean it's 'on'. The chat must then commence, and, well, this is where many a match goes awry. Everybody is different, but this is your chance to test your communication chemistry.

The importance of good, honest chat

While I don't think it's wise to use an app to procure pen pals, or to spend weeks chatting with a stranger without meeting them in the flesh, I do believe that the chat element of an app is integral to finding out whether you have more in common than your star signs and height difference. Consequently, it should never be skipped over. I personally place a lot of weight on effective communication, but even if conversation is not your jam, I do believe it's the first step in deciphering whether or not you have chemistry with someone, even if at this stage it's only on a purely communicative level.

You might be okay with one-word responses and unreciprocated questions, but this is a major turn-off for me. I'm so relieved when I can pick out the mismatched communicators in the early chat stages rather than having to wait until we're face to face to know that they haven't got anything interesting to say. For me, it's a way to establish a connection and, from there, decide whether or not to go on a date.

What is your intention? It's good to get clear about the purpose of conversing through an app. My intention is always super clear. I'm searching for three main things:

1. Do we have a similar sense of humour?
2. Are we going to have enough in common and enough differences to have things to talk about if we meet?
3. Are we here for the same reasons?

Your intentions might be completely different from mine, and that's fine as long as you're clear on what *your* intentions are. When you're not, you can spend countless hours going back and forth without really getting anywhere.

I urge you to use chatting on apps to move you forward in some way. Not to go for days asking how their weekend was and where they plan to travel on their next overseas trip, but to figure out whether or not this is the kind of person you want to meet in the flesh and share a drink/meal/first kiss with.

How this first stage of connection goes will differ for everybody, and I'm going to help you out here, because as a self-touted communication queen, I'm happy to pass my gifts on to you. But first, let's start with the trickiest sentence you'll ever write: the opening line!

Start strong

Every app is different. Some are geared towards women making the first move. Some are open to either party opening up the lines of communication as long as a match has been made. And others will allow you to message anyone regardless of whether you've even matched. I don't much like the latter type. They're reminiscent of the guy across the bar who persistently chats to you even after you've made it clear that you're not interested. I prefer to stick to the apps where women make the first move, which sounds empowering, but can also be freaking tricky! It made me really appreciate the pressure of making the first move that men have carried for eons. Note I said 'appreciate' not 'feel sorry for', because you know women have childbirth, periods and the gender pay gap, so a few witty opening one-liners ain't gonna kill them. Amirite?

Opening a conversation with 'Hey', 'Hi', 'Howdy' or 'Holla' is fine. But in a sea of other potential suitors, a reply that offers them zilch to work with except an identical response is not ideal. That's why, in the name of book research, I trialled a bunch of different openers on men, and also asked a select group of my single friends to trial a few on different men and women (only if they were interested in them, there was no insincere swiping happening – not on my watch, anyway).

These dos and don'ts were compiled based on a positive reply. Please note these are (unofficial) findings.

- ♥ *Do* personalise your opening line to the person you're initiating a conversation with. Comment on something they raised in their bio or included in their pictures. People can sniff out a reused opener a mile off.
- ♥ *Don't* think a string of cute emojis is clever or funny. It's not.
- ♥ *Do* ask a question so that they have something to respond with. It keeps the conversation flowing and takes the pressure off them.
- ♥ *Don't* use a template response from the app. It's lazy!
- ♥ *Do* inject your personality into your response where possible. Do you consider yourself funny? Let them know with a tasteful joke. Dad jokes fare particularly well, apparently.
- ♥ *Don't* start off with dirty talk unless you're on that kind of app (this was not me, but I feel like you knew that already.)

At this point I must let you in on a little secret: it's quite likely you won't receive a response from everyone you message, and that has NOTHING to do with you. These people don't know you. It's likely they dropped into a swipe frenzy in a moment of boredom. I know that when I take the time to craft a well-worded and witty conversation starter and it gets ignored a little piece of me dies inside. It's highly unlikely that their inability to respond has anything to do with their judgement of your word choice, their regret for swiping for you, or that they met someone who knows you and said, 'Keep your distance, she's crazy!' (this ran through my head once, but ridiculous).

It is part of the online dating experience, and yeah, it's shit, but know for sure that if they don't respond, they're not the person for you. It's as simple as that. There's no vibrational match and it's time to move on. Your personal vibration remains intact and you're not wasting your time with someone who's not interested in getting to know you.

But what happens if they do respond? Jackpot! Let's look at how to keep the conversation going.

Use your chat time wisely

I give good chat and have been told that I have a way with words, so there's a part of me that finds comfort in the volley of back-and-forth texting. I'm good at it. It's my strong suit. And I find it super sexy when someone can match my word-smithery. Maybe someone's ability to weave crafty words together isn't all that important to you. Perhaps you're not that great at it yourself. You don't want to be judged by your writing skills so choose not to judge someone else on theirs. Fair enough. But do use this time to decipher if it's worth putting on a nice outfit and brushing your hair for this person or whether you're just wasting your time and vibration on them. This is where friends of mine have slipped up. Sometimes, it's so exciting that someone is actually engaging with you that you say yes to a date without really working out if you're well suited. Ask the questions that you want answers to, but don't ask ALL the questions. You want to save something to talk about on a first date.

Essentially, what you're looking for is value alignment. You can be very subtle about finding this out, but this is your opportunity to gently peek into what their values are and see if they align with the ones you established in the first half of this book. To help you as you go sleuthing for their values, here are some things I like to broach in initial chat sessions:

- ♥ I ask them about their work. Not because their profession matters to me, but because I want to understand how they feel about the work they do. If they complain about it, disregard it or are confused by it, it's an indicator that perhaps they're not in vibrational alignment with me. I'm passionate about the work I do in the world, and I want my partner to have a similar passion for the work they do. I find that incredibly appealing.
- ♥ I ask them what they're excited about at the moment. Again, I want to know that they have things in their life that light them up.
- ♥ I watch out for negative talk around money. I am so done with a scarcity mentality. I'm not on the hunt for the next

billionaire, in fact, how much money they make isn't important to me at all. What is important to me is their relationship with money. I don't ask them about that outright (that would be rude). But if they're whining about not having enough money before we've even met, I'm super wary.

♥ I watch out for their ex-partners making cameos in the conversation in the early stages of chatting. It's unnecessary and, from experience, it's a big red flag that you're a rebound chat or that they've got some baggage they're still working through.

♥ I make sure my quirky sense of humour is showcased, just in case they don't get it. I'd much rather have my jokes shut down via messaging than when I'm sitting opposite them.

♥ I consider how one-sided the conversation is. If I'm the one asking all the questions and they're not asking any in return, it's an indication that the first date is going to be pretty much the same.

Some other topics you might like to consider exploring in your first chats:

♥ Outdoorsy? This is a good time to establish if they're more bookworm than Bear Grylls.

♥ Keen traveller? Some people are homebodies and don't like hopping on aeroplanes. Or perhaps their work, their kids or other commitments keep them glued to one place. It's a good time to establish whether or not your plans to be overseas for six months of the next year would actually suit them.

♥ Kids? If they haven't mentioned them in their profile and it's a deal-breaker for you, it's important to establish whether or not they have kids before you meet in real life. I get asked all the time if I have children and it used to piss me off. I was always like, 'Buddy, if I had kids I would have said so in my profile,' but then I spoke to a bunch of men and women who choose not to offer up that information because they're worried that people dismiss them too easily. That holds validity BUT they're going to find out eventually. It's better to ask up front if this is a deal-breaker for you.

♥ Living situation? I am not all that fussed how people live, but I do have a girlfriend who will not date men who live in share houses. She doesn't understand how anyone in their thirties can share a bathroom with someone who isn't blood related or sharing bodily fluids (her words, not mine). So, if you're anything like my girlfriend, it's good to establish these things early, but perhaps leave out the bodily fluids bit.

Once I feel I have achieved my intention and used my chat time wisely, I start to shift the conversation towards setting up a date (if they haven't already). If they don't take the bait, I'm out of there. If chatting has gone on longer than three days and a connection is yet to be established, it's unlikely it's going to materialise out of nowhere. Your limit may be longer or shorter than three days, but set one, trust me. Otherwise you're going to have a long list of pen friends and no actual dates (which is what we're here for, remember).

Setting up a date

As a seasoned dater (that sounds like a menu item, it's not) I have surmised that there are three first-date scenarios that are currently trending. We'll explore the ins and outs for the first date in the next chapter, but for now we're just setting the date up. Here are the three most common dating scenarios:

1. The coffee date

This is a really nice entry-level date. It requires very little time commitment and can take place in daylight and in public, so you have witnesses if things get weird. It's a nice transition from total strangers to 'Let's get to know each other'.

Pros: In and out. Great option if you're unsure of your date. Cheap and cheerful. No alcohol means there's ample opportunity to get an accurate sense of their energetic vibration without the crutch of a drink. Perfect if you don't drink and are not in the mood to explain to a stranger why.

Cons: Non-committal. Can feel like a test run. Could be a sign of a cheapskate.

Bottom line: I personally don't love the coffee date. To me, it screams, 'I don't want to spend any money on you so I'll spend $4 ($5 if you order an almond latte), and if it goes okay then I'll fork out a little more money.' HOWEVER, if I'm not sure about someone, it's a really easy way to not get stuck at dinner or drinks. In short, don't be offended if you're invited on one, they're commonplace. Initiate one if unsure about whether or not you want to date this person.

'I used to prefer a coffee date. Firstly, I don't drink, and secondly, I prefer the casual feel of a daytime catch-up. Also, if it goes well, you've got the option to take it into lunch or dinner depending on the time of day you meet. This is actually how my fiancé and I met. We connected on an app, met for a coffee at 10 am and ended up saying goodnight at 10 pm! Four years on, we're just about to get married.' – Jamie.

2. Meet for a drink

This is a definite step up from coffee. It usually requires a sacrifice of at least a portion of your evening, and let us not tiptoe around it, alcohol makes dating easier. I've been on 'meet for a drink' dates that have lasted an hour and some that have lasted 12 hours. The majority of the time, if it's going well, it will usually lead to dinner.

Pros: Alcohol settles the nerves (so does meditation; you're an adult, pick your poison). Drinks have the potential to lead to dinner with the option of parting ways if it isn't going well.

Cons: It's more of an investment than coffee. It requires putting a little effort into your appearance and can sometimes feel a bit harder to exit from than a quick coffee. If you don't drink alcohol, it can also raise questions you might not be ready to answer.

Bottom line: It's a safe option. It's not as 'all in' as a dinner date, but it still says 'I'm invested in spending time with you' more than a coffee date.

'I feel like there is so much you can learn about someone on a drink date. First of all, it helps me to relax and feel more comfortable. It helps the conversation flow a little easier but more importantly, it gives a little window into how they order, what they order, how they handle their alcohol, and allows them to relax a little, too.' – Morgan

3. Shall we grab dinner?

I have to say, I don't do many first dates that intentionally start as dinner, although most of my first-date drinks turn into dinner (not to brag).

Pros: A dinner date usually means they're keen. They also don't mind spending money on you. Dinner gives you a chance to find out if they love or hate coriander. (#makeorbreak)

Cons: It's a commitment. If you decide in the first ten minutes that you're not into them, you have to sit through three courses and then do the payment dance at the end.

Bottom line: Dinner dates are an opportunity to really get to know someone, but the consensus is that they're better reserved for the following scenarios: a drink date has progressed well, you've met before, or you're certain you guys are going to get on like a house on fire.

'I love a dinner date! It's an opportunity to really get to know someone in a setting that has lots of distractions for the hands like holding a wine glass, arranging your napkin, using cutlery like a civilised human. Lots of great ways to settle the nerves (and wandering hands). – Penny

Here are some other fun first-date ideas:

- ♥ **Dessert date.** Grab an ice-cream or hot chocolate and go for a walk. Good option if you don't want to drink and it can be done in the day or night.

- ♥ **Go for a walk.** I love this one, but also consider safety first. Probably not a wise idea to go on a 10-kilometre hike through dense bush with a stranger. Opt for a busy coastal walk or a stroll along the sand.

- ♥ **Markets.** I've actually had a few first dates at the farmers' markets. There is something quite revealing about shopping for vegetables with someone. Most markets will also have coffee, food stalls and live music. It's actually a really nice way to get to know somebody.

Close the loop

My dear friend and business and mindset coach, Rachel MacDonald, brought to my attention the notion of 'closing the loop'. She referenced it originally when it came to business and personal interaction. It included situations such as birthing an idea with a collaborator but never touching on it again, a conversation that started but never ended, or a carrot that was dangled but never dropped. Each scenario would leave the other party wondering, energetically open and without closure, answers or carrots. Closing the loop is a way to provide the other party (and yourself) with that closure.

The same applies to your interactions in the dating world, but never has it been more important than when it comes to the dating apps. I'll explore the phenomenon that is ghosting in chapter 11, but for now, know that not only is it good manners to intentionally close the loop on an app interaction, but it also enables an energetic closure of that interaction. As soon as you start engaging with someone, you're activating your vibrational field with theirs. If you choose to disengage, it's important that you deactivate that vibrational field by closing the loop.

Surprise success stories

At this juncture, I'd like to share some of my own 'successful' dating app swipes that surprised me. And by that, I mean I took a chance on someone I wouldn't usually swipe on and it resulted in some lovely dates (and, in some cases, relationships).

Surprise #1: Pete

Bio: Immature, brief, contained a surplus of emojis, mentioned pizza.

Details: 5 feet, 10 inches, Leo.

Pics: Varied, friendly, no selfies, attractive.

Pros: He was cute and a Leo.

Cons: Everything else. I must have been bored. I usually wouldn't swipe for someone with such a basic bio.

Story: You haven't met Pete, and he's not really worth mentioning past this scenario (sorry, Pete!). His profile was way below my usual standard: his bio was about pizza; he hadn't said shit about himself or his interests, and every photo was the same … yet I swiped. And not only did I swipe, I swiped knowing it would be an instant match. (Sometimes you just know this stuff!) It started with a playful initiating message, something to do with pizza, something not very me, something that screamed bored and not interested, yet it took one witty reply and I was in, hook, line and sinker. This approach doesn't work for all women. I take wit and clever humour over impressive job title, romance and definitely gym selfies (I really despise them). But admittedly, wit will still only take you so far. Pete's wit took him three weeks deep into nightly messages. We connected over his love of writing and my obsession with crime dramas (he was a criminal lawyer).

Summary: Pete had some baggage that doesn't need to be aired in a book written by a woman he dated a few times, but if his life had not been so 'complicated' when we met, then this would have been a great example of someone smart, witty, fun and interesting (and cute) not selling themselves well on an app. He was a bloody catch, even though his profile read 'Guy enjoys pizza'.

Surprise #2: Jack
Bio: Witty, cheeky, intelligent.
Details: 33 years old, 6 feet 3 inches tall, lived in the town I was moving to the following week, enjoyed wine, Virgo.
Pics: No selfies, varied, showed clear shot of face, clear shot of height, playing basketball, surfing, gave a good sense of style and dress sense.

Pros: Witty bio, varied activities, enjoyed a glass of wine, and lived in my new town.

Cons: VERY tall (I'm only 5 feet 4 inches), one year younger than me (so stupid, but it mattered at the time), appeared more 'good time' than 'love you long time' and, honestly, at that point I wasn't sure I could date a Virgo. (#ocd)

Story: We started chatting on a rainy Saturday afternoon. I was getting ready to move to a new town. There was instant banter, a matched intelligence and wit, and instant chemistry. We moved to texting that night and texted regularly throughout the week. The day I moved all of my furniture into my new house he brought over a bottle of wine and that was it. We dated for three months and then he left (but that's a story for later).

Summary: If we'd met in a pub, I probably wouldn't have looked twice at him, except maybe to point out the exceptionally tall guy. My first impression of him was definitely not the real representation of him. Because we'd spent a week chatting, our first date felt like our fifth. Our relationship, however brief, was definitely a kismet encounter. I cannot imagine having gone through life and not experiencing Jack, even if only for three months. He taught me incredible things about myself. And I truly believe an app was the only way we would have connected.

Surprise #3: Kurt

Bio: Interesting, detailed, accomplished, well written.

Details: 42, 6 feet tall, lived in a neighbouring town, looking for a relationship, wanted to have kids, Scorpio.

Pics: Varied, no selfies, friendly face, handsome, out with friends.

Pros: Intelligent, older man, ready to settle down, seemed legitimate in his search for love, different from other men I'd dated, interesting profession.

Cons: He was older than all the men I'd dated, he had a bit of a daggy vibe (but it was actually endearing) oh, and he was a Scorpio, but hey, who am I to judge? (#Gemini)

Story: We matched but I ran out of time to contact him (a downside of the app I was using) so he extended the match for 24 hours (this is an indicator that they are keen). We started chatting and his responses were considered, thoughtful and intelligent. He was a man of his word (he said he'd contact me the following night and he did). We arranged a first date. It was perfect. We laughed, shit got deep, he was respectful, and before the date ended, he arranged the second date. Now you roughly know the story of Kurt. He didn't end as one would have hoped (just as dating someone in the real world could go either way). But as far as meeting someone on an app could go it was a dream.

Summary: Kurt was not the guy for me. But the two months we did spend together getting to know each other was not an experience I would erase. Again, it's unlikely we would have met in other circumstances. We frequented different places and moved in different circles, and I'm not sure Kurt would have approached me in public, as he told me he would have assumed we'd have little in common.

What I've learned about apps: a memoir

If you're ready to date, and I mean seriously date, then you must get yourself on a dating app pronto. However, this comes with a caveat: you must work on strengthening your personal vibration first. People will ghost you. They'll quit responding to messages, leave you hanging, and downright ignore you, and this is way before they've met you. You can't take this stuff personally. They don't know you. You don't know them, or their circumstances. It took me a while to not take offence to the rejection of not matching, and not receiving a response to my well-thought-out messages and my clever responses to their questions.

But then I realised a valuable piece of information that changed the app dating game for me. The time you spend on an app is *not* dating. It's the pre-game warm-up. You can't allow the vetting process to affect your confidence or identity on the dating 'scene' because you're not at the dating bit yet. This person doesn't know you from a bar of soap (that turn of phrase makes no sense, but it seems fitting). I know my personality and energy far outshine my profile pictures and messages. So when someone rejects me based on my attempt to start a conversation with them, it doesn't allow for tone, lash bats, or an IRL cheeky smile. It's just plain silly of me to take offence.

I suggest you approach dating apps as a means to an end. They're a wonderful alternative to waiting in a bar patiently to be picked up (which as we've discovered is happening less and less). They give you a unique opportunity to meet a myriad of people who perhaps you wouldn't ordinarily have the chance to meet, and in what other context can you avoid opposing star signs without having to subtly ask when their birthday is? If you've had bad experiences in the past, I want you to try my 30-day app experiment on page 197. If you've never been on an app before I'm so excited for you to try it. And if you've been on them for years and are yet to find love, I reckon that's all about to change now that your personal vibration is in tip-top shape.

But before we start, here are four things to watch out for when using the apps (these are things I learned the hard way):

1. **The distance settings on dating apps are tricky little things.** They can fool you into thinking a hottie you've swiped right for is a local when he could be in your hood on business, on a boozy bucks weekend, literally driving through when you happen to be on the app, or worse he's in town for his own wedding (yes, it's happened to me before. One last look at what was out there perhaps?)! Always a good idea to check where they actually live.

2. **Apps are where the recently broken-hearted go to boost their ego.** This is a truth I discovered the hard way over and over again. The immediacy of an app match does the same thing to our serotonin levels as an Instagram or Facebook like. Instant gratification. And if you've ever been dumped or had your heart stomped on, you'll know that an ego boost is a much-sought-after high. How do you avoid this? Well, you can be super up front and ask them when their most recent relationship ended, or you can be a little more subtle and ask them how long they've been on the app, or why they're on the app (but without being intrusive;

I know it's tricky but will save you in the long run). They're not always going to be honest, I get it, but I just wanted to forewarn you because I've counselled MANY a heartbroken man on our first date (one of my least favourite superpowers is making people feel so comfortable on dates that they share their heart and soul with me in the first hour of meeting). Kinda ruins the mood.

3. **Swiping is a competitive sport.** Some people use apps as a time-waster. They swipe with zero intention of actually going out on a date. They get the serotonin hit when they match (see above) but that's all they're there for. I've been guilty of this in the past. Don't be this person, and if you don't hear from somebody, know that this type of person exists.

4. **'Casual' does not mean 'until I find the one'.** You're going to come across a bunch of people who want 'something casual'. Believe them when they say this. Please don't go in thinking you're going to be the one to change their mind and make them want a relationship. They've been honest with you, now you just need to be honest with yourself.

Exercise 19

THE 30-DAY APP EXPERIMENT

Confession! I pulled 30 as the number of days out of my bottom. Basically, I want you to spend an entire month implementing these strategies, just as an experiment. It might take you longer than 30 days to land a hot date, it might take you less time, either way I want you to stick to the experiment for at least a 30-day period.

Setting up your profile

♥ Create an honest bio that reflects your personality.

♥ Choose recent pictures of yourself that include you relaxed and smiling, one full body shot, no filters, and that reflect your personality. Give them a snapshot of who you are today (not you pre-haircut).

♥ Most apps offer you an opportunity to declare why you're on the app, e.g. Looking for a relationship. Make sure this is ticked. Owning why you're there is always going to be an asset. And it cuts through the bullshit of people who are just there for a booty call misinterpreting your messages.

Swiping

♥ Don't swipe mindlessly. Read profiles, examine pics.

♥ See if you can tap in to their energy. A natural, candid shot combined with an honest bio is a key indicator of someone's energy. Try swiping based on this alone for a few days and see how you go.

>>

>>

♥ Do not judge on clothing choice, food preference or star sign. At the end of the day this stuff isn't nearly as important as the weight we give it and it certainly doesn't define a person. Unless you have their entire astrological natal chart you can't make a judgement (once you know what sign their Venus is in then judge away).

♥ Every day swipe right for someone you wouldn't ordinarily choose to swipe for. Of course, be discerning with this, but perhaps it's someone who's not your usual 'type' or perhaps they have a profession that you don't think would make a good match. Perhaps you can overlook the reference to *Simpsons* quotes or grammatical errors (I mean, I couldn't ignore the grammar but maybe you can). Also, if there are a bunch of people you feel are out of your league, definitely swipe for these people. Basically, take yourself outside your swiping comfort zone.

♥ Dedicate ten minutes twice a day to swiping and then stay out of the app for the rest of the day. Trust me. If you only swipe with intention you will get much better results.

♥ If you match, instigate conversation. Don't let a match pass you by. I am a terrible culprit with this. I match all the time and very rarely open up the conversation. Not only is this bad manners but, ahem, how are you going to get a date if you don't take the next step?

Chatting

♥ Again, for emphasis, do open up the chat with everyone you match with.

♥ Use this time wisely but also set yourself a time limit for chatting.

♥ Find out what matters to them. Ask them what excites them about their upcoming week. You can't define people by what they do for work, but you can get a peek into who they are by working out what lights them up.

♥ See if you can find aligned values through the questions you ask. This will get easier to do once you're on a date, but it doesn't hurt to throw in some questions early.

♥ Notice how your vibration shifts when you're talking to them. Don't judge, just observe. This is important and good practice for when you do meet.

♥ If you'd like to take it further, suggest a date. Women can absolutely make the first move on a dating app (and IRL). In fact, the fellas love it.

♥ Once a date has been set, exchange phone numbers. Take it off the app. The app's purpose has been served.

The date

♥ Choose somewhere you feel safe.

♥ Always tell someone where you're going and at what time.

♥ Only consent to things you feel comfortable with. You can change your mind at any time.

♥ Check in with your personal vibration at all times, but don't mistake nerves and discomfort for a weak vibration.

>>

>>

The extras

♥ If you lose interest at any stage, feel like they're not actually suited or perhaps you've connected strongly with someone else, close the goddamn loop. By this I mean don't leave them hanging, don't disappear and don't leave them wondering what they did wrong.

♥ Interact with more than one person at a time. This is completely acceptable and it spreads your energy around a little bit. If you're focusing all of your energy on one person at the app stage, it can be disappointing when it doesn't work out. I reiterate, you are not dating yet. It is a vetting process. At the match and chat stage you can talk to as many people as you like (as long as you close the loop).

If you give apps a go and you decide they're not for you, that's absolutely fine. I get it. I float in and out of my own use of them, but I still stand by my original statement that they are THE most efficient way to line up an actual date.

That stranger might just be a lover you haven't met yet

I was never given the 'Don't talk to strangers' spiel as a kid. In fact, I think Mum would have loved it if I had half the confidence that she had to strike up a conversation with someone I wasn't already acquainted with. Her ability to become friends with everybody she met was something that embarrassed and mortified me growing up, but I really admire it now.

I'm not going to walk you through the process of meeting a stranger step by step the way I did for the section about dating apps. There's not much to say. But know this: everyone is a stranger until they're not, and so it's time we smiled more, held eye contact and struck up a conversation with the hottie at the local coffee shop, because if it's not the barista you fall in love with, it might be his mate, or his sister's work friend, or his colleague, or ... you get the picture.

The magic of engaging with a stranger comes down to widening your energetic field. Being open to people outside the confines of the social circles in which you move not only increases your chances of meeting someone, it also exposes you to people you wouldn't necessarily encounter – just like the apps do.

If you're an introvert, you are most likely breaking into cold sweats at the thought of striking up a conversation with someone you don't know, but as an introvert myself I'm here to say it can be a lot more subtle than that.

How often do you avert your eyes when someone attempts to make eye contact with you? What would happen if you didn't? What if you held their gaze and smiled – what energy would shift then, do you think? I trialled this over a 48-hour period just for fun. I didn't meet my soulmate, but I did return the smile of a guy in Woolies who later helped me carry my overflowing and wildly heavy basket to the self-checkout (anyone else refuse to get a trolley even though you're doing a massive shop?). Chivalry is, indeed, alive.

I also held eye contact with a man in the bookstore (I know, such a cliché) and he came over to ask me if I had any good book recommendations for his wife's birthday. Okay, so probably not the best example, but it does demonstrate the possibilities that open up when you stretch your energy a little further than your comfort zone.

What my 48-hour experiment made me realise is how often I look down, avert my eyes, or pretend I haven't seen a person in order to avoid an awkward conversation. Sometimes, this unintentionally gets misconstrued as me being not only uninterested but also rude.

A fella I once had a crush on told me recently that he kept seeing me everywhere, but that I never looked at him. 'I just assumed you hated me,' he said. A little part of me died and thought, *HATED YOU? I was in love with you!* Don't be me. He's now married with two gorgeous children who wear earthy-toned linens and look like they've popped out of a kids' clothing catalogue.

Once you actually start smiling back, making eye contact, introducing yourself and just being plain old-fashioned friendly, you'll be widening your energetic field and strengthening your personal vibration. Even if nothing comes of it initially, you're increasing your potential for connection.

FELICIA AND TONY: WRONG DRINK, RIGHT GUY

Felicia had never enjoyed music festivals. It wasn't an aversion to live music that deterred her; it was more about the crowds, the long days and the excessive sloppiness of her particular group of friends. It was her best friend Claire's birthday, however, and Felicia knew that putting her feelings aside was the right thing to do when Claire begged her to attend this festival with her. The morning of the festival, Felicia wondered what excuse she could use to stand up Claire. There were five other friends going so surely she wouldn't be too disappointed if an unexpected migraine or period pain or heart condition surfaced. But when Claire sent an *I'M SO EXCITED* text, Felicia knew she was trapped.

When the group arrived at the festival it was all of ten minutes before Claire ran off into a sea of music fans, and Felicia found herself separated from the group. She decided to make the most of the day by enjoying the live music from a safe distance, away from the mosh pits. After waiting nearly an hour in line at the bar, ordering a vodka mixer and being handed a beer, she questioned whether this was a sign to just leave.

Felicia stumbled out of the queue of drinkers holding a beer she was never going to drink and saw a guy sitting under a tree on his own, opening the vodka mixer she'd had her eye on. When she asked him if he'd swap her that drink for the beer, he looked up, smiled and said he'd been waiting for a beer and had also been given the wrong drink. They swapped drinks on condition that they'd drink them together. Tony and Felicia sat under that tree all day until the sun went down. Turned out that they'd both been dragged there by friends and neither of them were interested in getting lost in the crowds. At the end of their time together, Tony turned to her and said, 'I was regretting coming to this festival and was about to leave in a huff after the beer mix-up, but all of it was worth it to have met you.'

Have you met my single friend?

If you really want to know what a friend thinks of you, ask them to set you up with someone.

I have been on several blind dates that have been set up by friends. In most cases, I have to say it's been somewhat insulting because, let's be frank, the number-one reason a friend sets you up with another friend is that you're both single. 'Oh, I know just the guy/gal for you,' they say. 'You two are sooo similar.'

The only thing me and the narcissistic horserace caller had in common was the fact that we were both recovering from becoming recently (and unexpectedly) single. The only thing I had in common with the professional skateboarder was that he was looking for a rebound and I happened to be unattached. And the only thing I had in common with Gina's husband's boss's second cousin was that we were the only two single people at the wedding.

Don't let me put you off dating a friend of a friend, because as terrible as my particular track record is, most surveys you come across online that attempt to work out the most successful way of meeting a significant other, all come back with 'through friends'. This is very promising, don't you think? I do believe that if done in the right way it always helps to have a glowing reference from a pal whose opinion of others you trust implicitly.

MEGAN AND DAN: MEANT TO BE

Megan had just started stocking her natural perfumes in Chelsea's store in town. After several drop-offs and little effort, they soon became friends. One day Chelsea floated the idea of setting up Megan with her flatmate, Dan. 'Nooo,' said Megan, 'absolutely not'. But Chelsea was convinced they needed to meet. Sure, they had quite a bit in common: they were both non-drinkers, they were both old souls and nature lovers, but more than that Chelsea just knew they'd love each other. Still Megan said, 'NO!'

Unbeknown to Megan, Dan also had reservations about this unsolicited set-up. 'She seems too woo-woo; I've dated types like her before.' Reluctantly, Chelsea let it go. Then one day, Megan was dropping off stock to the store and having her regular catch-up with Chelsea when Dan walked in. Chelsea's face lit up at the kismet timing of this. She hadn't even orchestrated it.

Dan and Megan knew they had each rejected Chelsea's invitation to set them up, so although the initial introduction was slightly awkward, they both had an overwhelming sense of familiarity. A hello soon turned into a four-hour conversation. Six months later, they were living together, and two years on they're in an incredibly supportive, mutually respectful and surprisingly well-matched relationship.

RITA AND PAUL: NAN KNEW IT

Rita wasn't looking to be set up, but after several friends mentioned Paul and what a good match they would be, she agreed to a blind date with him, but only if a couple of her friends joined them. Paul was a teacher (so was Rita) and he was tall, dark and handsome – so she'd been told.

You see, this set-up took place before social media and mobile phones were a thing, so she was literally going in blind. A week before the date, Rita's nan pulled her aside. 'Your mum said you're going on a blind date next week. Make sure you go. You won't want to go, but make sure you do. He's the one.' Nan had always been a little psychic.

On the night of the date, Rita was uncharacteristically nervous – so much so that en route to the restaurant she swung the car around and headed home. But then she remembered what her nan had said. She knew she would regret it if she didn't at least turn up to see what he looked like. The minute Rita saw Paul she could feel the energy between them. The friends who had accompanied them both to cushion the first-date jitters had left when they realised that Rita and Paul were completely enamoured of each other.

They saw one another every single day after that and were married a year later. They've now been married 27 years, and have three children and one grandchild. Rita believes that their union was divinely orchestrated, but she also knows that without the persistence and glowing recommendations from her friends and the wise words from her nan, she'd never have met Paul.

You might be reading these true love stories and thinking, *I know all my friends' single friends, and I don't want to touch any of them with a ten-foot pole.* I hear you! BUT I want you to open your mind a little. This isn't about saying yes to every awkward set-up your friends attempt because they feel it's their civic duty to get you 'off the market'. It's about accepting invitations to friends' barbecues, dinner parties and impromptu gatherings, knowing that you are widening your energetic field by meeting new people. When you're surrounded by people your friend likes for one reason or another, this generally (though not always, let's be honest) means that you'll feel a connection with them, too. If you still need convincing ...

♥ Group settings take the pressure off big time!
♥ Hopefully your friends have good taste in friends. I mean, they're friends with you after all and you're pretty great!
♥ You might just make another great friend, and did you know that a huge percentage of relationships start as a platonic friendship?
♥ It gets you off the apps! (But you love those now anyway, don't you?)

Exercise 20

THE 30-DAY FRIENDS EXPERIMENT

If you want to be *actually* dating, which I have been very clear is our intention here, then here is another crazy experiment. I want you to put your 'I can't be bothered' feelings to one side and accept all invitations for another 30-day period. Think of this as your very own *Yes Man* response to meeting someone.

>>

\>\>

- ♥ **If your friend suggests a set-up, agree to it!** But first, ask them why they think you'll be a good match. If the only thing you have in common is that you're both single, approach with caution. If your friend can list a few legitimate reasons why they think you should meet this person, then absolutely go for it.
- ♥ **If you get invited to after-work drinks, go.** You can always leave if you aren't feeling the vibe. Just make sure you ask your work friends to introduce you to people you don't know.
- ♥ **If your mate throws an impromptu Sunday barbecue and insists you come, instead of making your usual excuses ask, 'What would you like me to bring?'** Friends' gatherings are safe because, well, your friends will be there. And what's the worst thing that can happen? You make some new friends? Always go.

When I did this experiment myself (because that's only fair, right?), I was surprised how often I used to turn opportunities down. Once I started saying yes, I discovered connections begging to be made. Did I find my sweetheart? No. But I did go on a date that several friends set up thinking that we'd make a perfect match. They weren't wrong. We had a bunch in common; he was funny, engaging and intelligent, but there was just no spark. BUT he's honestly become one of my favourite people to hang out with, and I don't regret the experience for a second.

Every opportunity you get to be out in the real world parading your personal vibration around is valuable. If you allow it to, every dating experience can teach you more about what it is you desire and how it is you want to feel in a relationship.

Other ways to land a hot date

♥ **Do more of the things you love.** Join a ceramics class, a local sporting team or a new fitness studio, or go to your favourite comic convention. Enjoying hobbies that you love is going to have your personal vibration firing, and it's likely that you'll meet people who are equally passionate about the things you are, if you're out actually doing those things.

♥ **Volunteer!** This was suggested to me by a friend and I love it. Want to meet someone with similar values to yours? Make sure you're out there living your values day to day.

♥ **Borrow a cute puppy and go to the dog park.** I was puppy minding for a month and have never been hit on by so many men in my life. FYI the bigger the dog the more powerful the (man) magnet.

♥ **Attend a singles event.** Oh, I know, so cringey, but I think singles events have come a long way in recent years. They're fun and well thought out, and at least you know that everyone in the room is there for the right reasons. I see singles events as online dating in real life. So if your issue with meeting someone on an app is that you can't feel their energy through your phone, this is your opportunity to tune in to the energy of an entire room full of singles.

♥ **Go out solo.** This seems counterintuitive but hear me out. It's scary AF approaching someone in public when they're surrounded by a horde of friends. I often work from cafés and end up in conversations with the guy doing the same thing at the table next to me. But if you don't work from your laptop, never fear, there are other options. Take a book or a journal, or simply people watch. Try to keep your face out of your phone, and make sure you smile at people. (I feel like your mother. Have you got a jacket?)

♥ **Go on an adventure.** People have told me countless stories while writing this book of couples meeting on Contiki tours or hiking through the Andes, falling in love on the deck of a cruise ship or waiting for a flight at the airport, and in one particularly cute story they ended up sharing a double-booked hotel room when the rest of the hotel was booked out. As a well-versed solo traveller, I promise you it's impossible not to meet new people, and it does wonders for really fine-tuning your personal vibration.

Hopefully this chapter has made you a little braver, a tad more open and hopeful about meeting someone. Remember, at this stage we're just setting up a date. You're not committed, and you're most definitely not locked into anything. It doesn't have to be the start of your happily ever after. We're simply getting you out on actual dates for you to road test your new personal vibration, and see what an asset you are to a potential suitor.

You didn't think I was going to help you land that hot date and not give you my epic guide to navigating the first few dates, did you? Read on, my friend ...

- Chapter 10 -

Your complete guide to the first and second date

You've landed the hot date. (Go you.) Now it's time to actually physically go out and date. If first dates scare the crap out of you, buckle up, because I'm about to change your (dating) life. Your thoughts, feelings and now your actions are all pointing you in the right direction. The Law of Action is about to swing into high gear. It's time to take things offline and into real life.

I can't recall many first dates I've been on that haven't gone well. Sure, there's the odd 'No way, no how' pops up when a date organised on an app doesn't live up to their profile. Or there are those times when your date tells you the harrowing story of how their ex of 13 years had an affair with their best friend and now she's pregnant and he's not sure he has a right to be angry with them. He does love them after all. 'What do you think?' he asks, 45 minutes into dinner. And there have definitely been plenty of dates where I haven't felt any kind of connection whatsoever. But all in all, first dates are not the thing you should be wary of; second dates are what you need to watch out for!

First dates ain't got nothing on second dates, because that's when it can all turn to shit (but don't worry, I've got you). The good news is if you make it past the second date, then dates three, four and five are much of a muchness.

First Date 101

I remember rocking up to a first date with this guy ... Oh, wait. You met him a few chapters back. It was Nick (what a tool!). When I sat down at the bar Nick had invited me to, he proceeded to spend the first ten minutes of our date telling me, and I quote, 'This isn't a date, it's an interview process – all dates are a process of working out whether or not you like the person enough to want to spend the next drink with them.' At the time, I was appalled (although that ended up being the least appalling thing about him). Even though he could have used a bit more tact, Nick wasn't wrong. At least not entirely. First dates are your opportunity to do a few things:

Test out your new strengthened personal vibration. Does this person strengthen or weaken your vibration? Red flags don't always pop up on the first date. But if they do, don't feel like you need to push through it.

Get to know someone. I'm going to go through some questions you might like to ask on the first date in a bit, because first dates are your opportunity to find out about who this person is and whether you want to spend more time with them.

See how they communicate. First dates can be nerve-racking and so we can't judge someone's communication style on the first date alone, but ask yourself if they listened and asked interesting questions or if they just waited for you to finish talking so they could ask the next question on their predetermined list. This could be an indicator that they're not interested in your answer, they're just invested in asking their next question. Or it could also mean that they're nervous, so just note it for now.

Consider how you feel in their company. Do you feel safe, curious and happy? Or do you feel uncomfortable, defeated and inferior? These early feelings aren't defining, it's still early days, but definitely something to take note of.

I think the best piece of advice I can give you about your first date is to spend less time thinking, *Will they like me?* and more time thinking, *Do I like them?* And, *Is this somebody I want to spend more time with?* If you rock up to a date with a strong personal vibration, you won't need to think about impressing them; the right person will be attracted to your vibration. And if they're not? Well, they're not the person for you! See the simplicity? When your personal vibration is strong, you're being your authentic self. And THIS is who you want them to connect with, not the version of you that you *think* they want to connect with. Make sense?

I wish I'd known that vital piece of information when I first started dating. I used to spend first dates hoping the guys liked me without even contemplating whether I was interested in them. And often, I would end up in a relationship with someone completely unsuited to me, someone who, if I thought about it, I didn't even really like. Can you relate?

First-date fantasies

We all have these. I honestly try not to fall down the rabbit hole that is my wandering mind, but there is so much potential and possibility when sitting down to get to know someone properly. I start thinking, *Could they be the one? Will I feel that spark? Should I cancel my travel plans in December in case he invites me to his parents' place for Christmas lunch?*

Again, getting carried away with a storyline that isn't written yet is completely normal, but if we go back to the love stories we run and consider the potential damage they can do to our romantic future by skewing what we think we're worthy of and deserve, fantasies aren't any different. There's still room for them – I'm not a total killjoy – but when it comes to a first date, the best thing you can do is think of it as an opportunity to determine whether or not there's a vibrational connection. The only way to do that is by:

♥ Staying in the present moment. Future fantasies have no place on a first date.
♥ Being your authentic self. But if that includes belching at the table and pointing out people's flaws, perhaps save that for a few dates down the track.
♥ Initiating conversation that engages them and allows you to find out more about who they are.

Pre-date prep

I'm not about to rattle off a list of practices and procedures that you need to complete before going on your first date, but I have found a few things that help me feel more at ease before a date. Perhaps they'll work for you, too.

Pick a great venue

I prefer to be somewhere I've been before, but I try not to go somewhere I frequent all the time. There's nothing more annoying than being on a date where you're being watched by the entire waitstaff and the person you're with keeps stopping to talk to mates who've wandered in.

Make choosing the outfit stress-free

Have a few first-date outfit options on hand at all times. Things that make you feel comfortable, make you feel like yourself and are not unlike something you'd wear on a night out with friends. Having go-to outfits prevents you slipping into a meltdown minutes before you're meant to be there. Also, dress for *you*, not for your date, because if you're feeling uncomfortable in what you're wearing, you're going to spend the entire date fidgeting, rearranging your clothes and wanting to go to the bathroom to check that you still look like you did when you left the house. And that's no fun for anyone.

Try an energetic clearing

This tip won't be for everyone, but I always like to do an energetic clearing on myself before I leave the house. I take some time to sit in stillness, close my eyes and imagine a beautiful white light flowing through my body from the crown of my head to the tip of my toes. This white light clears any fear or anxiety, and I also always ask it to protect me while on the date.

Set an intention

What is your intention for this date? To meet someone new? To see if there's a connection? To find someone to have a relationship with? To have a bit of fun? All of these are perfectly legitimate and worthy intentions, but the key is to get clarity about your specific intention. Be wary of intentions that aren't coming from a good place. If you're dating to distract yourself from recent heartbreak, to prove you've still got 'it' or to make yourself feel sexy, worthy or beautiful, these are not good reasons to be going out on a first date, ya hear me?

Check in with your personal vibration

I always like to do a little inventory of my personal vibration before going out on a date. You can do this by going through the following steps:

♥ **Remind yourself of your core values.** You wrote these down in chapter 2. It's so easy to let your values fly out the window when you really want to connect with someone. But honestly, if you go in knowing exactly what your core values are, you'll be surprised at how quickly you notice when someone else is in alignment with them and when they're not.

♥ **Check in with your values about love.** You discovered yours in chapter 7. You may not get an opportunity to check these off on the first date, but it never hurts to go in with a reminder of what they are.

♥ **Tune in to the feelings you wish to radiate in a relationship.** You wrote these down in chapter 7. I like to sit in stillness (you can do this after an energetic clearing if you like) and feel the feelings I desire to radiate in that present moment. If this seems like a bit of a stretch for you, familiarise yourself with those feelings so you can recognise if they come up during your date.

♥ **Remind yourself that you're no longer following your old love story.** You wrote a new love story in chapter 7 (that was a productive chapter, right?). Your past baggage needn't apply here. Your new story means this date is going to be a totally new experience.

Prepare a story from your day to share

I've never been on a date where the first ten minutes of small talk didn't start with 'How was your day?' My response used to be the same (whether it was true or not): 'It was good. Busy.' I guess I thought that made me sound important. These days, I go in with a funny or light-hearted story from my day. It breaks the ice, opens up the conversation and always seems to put my date at ease. Trust me, I'm a professional (dater). Your story doesn't have to be outrageous; if you don't have one, just say something more than your standard cookie-cutter response.

Conversation starters

When it comes to dating, I have a gift and a flaw rolled into one: I am a rockstar communicator. As a trained journalist, it's very rare that I run out of questions to ask or conversational avenues to explore, and although that might sound like a wonderful trait, sometimes, on a first dates it works against me in two ways. Firstly, my expert probing means that my dates often start revealing parts of themselves and their pasts too soon – details that really should have been reserved for dates five, six and seven. Secondly, quite often, so much info is spilled on the first date that when date two comes around, it's filled with a bunch of awkward silences, or, worse, there is no date two because they're probably a little embarrassed by all that they've revealed.

Now, of course, there are a few different factors at play here. Without tooting my own horn, I do have a knack for making people feel at ease – like they can tell me anything. I adore the fact that my dates feel comfortable enough to tell me about their parents' divorce when they were eight years old or the reasons they believe their last relationship ended. But there's a time and a place for conversations like this, and, honestly, it's not on the first date. It's wonderful to ask questions and be interested in the person, but dating should not be an interrogation. It's also not an interview (as Nick so eloquently called it); it's your opportunity to get to know someone, and them you. Once I realised this, I began to leave space (yes, silence) for them to jump in with questions of their own.

If conversation doesn't come easily to you, you might find the following conversation starters quite helpful. Not just because they'll give you something to say and invite your date to open up, but also because the following prompts will allow you to find out more than who their favourite band is or where they went to school (yawn).

These prompts are in no particular order and they're just to get the ball rolling. Being authentic to yourself is the number-one goal on your first date, so rattling off all of my questions isn't the answer. But if you get stuck, these will help. And please, ALWAYS prioritise the flow of conversation over hitting all of the questions on your list. Listening and responding to the information they've given you is the key to connection and fluid conversation. Also, make sure you change these prompts to suit the person and the situation. Think of them as inspiration rather than your Cliffs Notes, and, whatever you do, don't take this book out on the date with you. (Imagine!)

What was the most exciting thing about your day?

Instead of just asking them how their day was, you're now enquiring about the things that light them up and get them excited. It also offers an opportunity for them to reciprocate the question. Best have your answer ready.

What's something about you that surprises people?

I always find this question interesting. It's less about the surprising thing and more about why it is something that they don't reveal to people. It's also inviting them to be a little vulnerable.

What's your biggest challenge with the work you do?

It's great to hear about the things that people enjoy but I always find it really interesting to know what they find difficult and how they deal with difficult situations.

What do you enjoy about the work you do?

You can't define someone by the work they do, but it's always interesting to know what they enjoy about their profession. Sometimes it has little to do with the role itself and more to do with the qualities they bring to the role. I love this question, and I love when people ask me this.

Where did you grow up?

This question sounds basic, but it opens up the conversation to learn about their family, their childhood, their relationships with their siblings, if they're new in town, and, if not, why they've never left. You feel me? Questions that open up conversation are gold, because it starts to feel less like that job interview and more like, ya know, an actual conversation.

What's your idea of a good life?

This is probably my favourite question. This will give you an opportunity to ask yourself if you resonate with the things that are going to make them happy.

What was the last book you read?

If you're not a reader and don't care either way if your partner reads, leave this one out or replace it with a movie, TV series, etc. I always ask this question, because I'm always looking for good book recommendations, plus I also love hearing about new things and having people explain why they're into them.

If you could get away with a crime, what would you do?

Again, this might not be your cuppa tea, but I love asking this question. It makes people squirm in their seat a little and always elicits a pretty interesting (sometimes curious) answer. I used to make a joke on dates ('used to' being the operative words) when people asked me what crime I would commit. I would say, 'Well, I'd probably murder someone. Oh, don't worry, they'd deserve it, and then I'd see if all of the hours I've spent watching British crime dramas paid off when I tried to dispose of the body.' Sometimes I'd get the laugh I was hoping for, but other times I'd feel the energy shift. Now I save that comedic bit for date four or five. You decide when it feels appropriate (if ever)!

The most important thing to keep in mind when it comes to conversation starters is that the point is to start a conversation. If you ask a question that ends in a one-off response it's called a Q&A, and eventually you'll run out of new things to ask. There's a difference between a pause and a comfortable silence, and literally having nothing left to ask. Ask open questions (ones that require more than a yes or no answer) and listen to their response. From here your next question can be based on the intricacies of their answer.

Personally, I love me some silence on a date. It never makes me feel awkward. I actually feel super comfortable with breaks in conversation. I put it down to having a strong personal vibration. It's only awkward if you make it awkward, and a person who can comfortably sit in silence earns themselves some massive brownie points.

Relax, what's the worst that can happen?

Hopefully you're not sick of hearing about your personal vibration yet, because honestly, if you work on strengthening yours, then there is absolutely nothing that can happen on a first date that you can't handle. Let's go through some hypothetical horror scenarios to put your mind at ease.

You don't connect. So what? Thank U, next! No, okay, sorry. That's insensitive. If you don't connect though, it's totally fine. In fact, it's good that you're able to establish that on the first date. Nobody is locking you in to a second date, and you get to leave with your personal vibration intact.

It's terrible and you want to leave midway through. If your date is being inappropriate or nasty, or making you uncomfortable, leave! You can absolutely do that, and I'll be cheering you on from the sidelines. You'll find that when you have a strong personal vibration, you'll pick up on this bad behaviour pretty quickly. If you're just not feeling a connection, then finish your drink or coffee or meal and politely leave.

You embarrass yourself. I'll start off by telling you an embarrassing story of my own, so nothing you ever do will compare. (This took place pre-COVID-19 by the way, so don't come at me for poor pandemic etiquette.) I was recovering from a cold and hadn't been out of the house for two weeks. I'd been waiting for this guy to ask me out for a while (we met through mutual friends) and he'd finally contacted me. I felt mostly fine though still a little sniffly, but there was no way I was missing out on this opportunity. I raced out the door and forgot to throw some tissues in my bag even though I had been repeating, *Don't forget the tissues*, in my head the entire day. Just as I was about to walk into the bar to meet him, I felt my nose run, and because I'm a classy gal, I wiped my nose with my wrist and proceeded to enter the bar.

The date was going okay, and after about an hour, I excused myself to go to the bathroom. Well, what a freaking surprise I got when I was washing my hands and looked in the mirror to not only see dried up snot sitting on the edge of one of my nostrils but also a fluorescent green booger sitting on my cheek! Honestly, it was beyond disgusting and such a turn-off, and also WHY HADN'T HE SAID ANYTHING?!

I contemplated catapulting myself out the bathroom window and making my escape down the back alley, but decided it was better to attack this head-on. So I cleaned myself up, headed back to the table and asked him whether I should judge him for the fact that he didn't feel the need to let me know that I looked like the snotty kid we all avoided in second grade. He laughed and said he didn't want to embarrass me. I made it into a joke. And we moved on.

So you embarrass yourself, so what? I'm not sure what catastrophic event you're playing out in your mind, but it's unlikely to happen. And if it does, big whoop. We're all adults. If your date is a decent human being, it won't matter, and if they're not, well, you'll know up-front, and that's the greatest gift you could ask for.

Bonus first-date advice

If you've got a case of the first-date jitters, you feel a flush rushing to your cheeks and a stutter stumbling from your lips, take a deep breath, read the following list and remind yourself of my embarrassing green booger story to induce laughter.

- ♥ There's nothing to be afraid of. You're not emotionally invested on the first date, unless you've spent two months conversing before meeting (don't do that), so walking away if you're not into them is okay, and any disappointment you feel if they're not into you will be fleeting.
- ♥ Do be aware that people are usually on their best behaviour on a date (except Nick, he was just an asshole). It's likely that you will be, too. This isn't an encouragement to be suspicious AT ALL, but just something to keep in mind.
- ♥ If you're feeling nervous, you can almost guarantee that your date is nervous, too. So be generous. If someone is

talking a lot or not talking at all, remember that it could be nerves. That said, I do believe that you're still able to pick up on someone else's energy and how it's affecting your personal vibration.

♥ Do you have a list of deal-breakers? Now is the time to bring them up. If religion is important to you, it's important to raise questions earlier rather than later. If you don't want to date someone who has children, it's important to make sure that any kids are out in the open, so to speak. If you could never date an over-user of gifs, trust me, now is the time to enquire about gif usage!

♥ Never keep your phone on the table, it's rude. If you need to check it, excuse yourself and go to the bathroom.

♥ Don't judge them on things that don't matter. We addressed this when we talked about dating apps. Honestly, if you don't like the shirt he chose or the way he holds chopsticks or the drink he ordered, let it go! It's easy to be picky on a first date, but if you're serious about finding a meaningful relationship, his gingham shirt is not a good reason to say no to a second date.

First date down, now let's reflect

I'm the very last person who is going to tell you to analyse, scrutinise and re-enact your first date over and over again. Trying to draw meaning from every word uttered, hand gesture made or lip bitten, is futile and unproductive. However, I do think some personal first-date reflection is helpful, and it's as simple as this: ask yourself, *How do I feel?*

It might help to write your feelings down or it might be enough to simply identify what they are. There is no need to analyse them, but it's helpful to not get caught up in the minutiae of the date by wondering things like, *What did it mean when he said that? Was I funny enough? Why did he keep scratching his head every time I asked a question?* Instead, focus on how you feel after spending time with this person.

In Part One you worked out how you felt when your personal vibration was strengthened and when it was weakened. It might be hard to tell after just one date, but it is worth checking in at this point to see if your personal vibration has been affected. My theory is that if we lovingly observe this along the way, then we're unlikely to be blindsided five months into a relationship and thinking, *How on earth did we end up together?*

Second time's a charm (or not)

Ah, the ever-elusive second date. It feels like you've jumped over the first hurdle; you've likely built up a rapport with them and it's a bloody relief to be past the small talk. But without the routine questions and the niceties that come with a first date, the second date can leave you both a little exposed. Do you actually have anything in common? Did you both run out of things to talk about on the first date? How will your personal vibration fare on the second encounter? The second date is your opportunity to determine if you have a genuine connection.

You see, you could send me on a first date with anyone and I'd be able to convince them it has been a success. Not through any insincerity, but because I love getting to know people and, as mentioned earlier, I can ask questions until the cows come home. But, often, by date two all the surface-level questions have been asked and it's time to dive a little deeper. I usually hold back a little on the second date, to allow my date to initiate questions (only because I'm such a question hog), and in many hilarious circumstances I have been dumbfounded at how easily we end up in precariously silent waters without me steering the conversational ship.

I dated this one guy for a few weeks, and I thought things were going well until I realised that I always guided the conversation. We laughed together because I was the one making all the jokes and we never ran out of things to talk about because I never let us. Over breakfast one morning, I decided to stay silent and only speak when spoken to (near impossible, but I did it). We literally sat in silence for an hour and a half. No joke! I ended it the next day. I was having a relationship with myself, and the truth is I could make myself laugh without him in the picture.

Clearly, as I keep mentioning, conversation is important to me. If it's not a big deal for you, then don't feel you need to test the waters in this way. But after that painful breakfast, I knew that I had to try not to initiate all the conversation if I was going to work out whether we got on really well or if it was another day working as a journo.

Tips for the second date

I'm not going to give you a step-by-step guide to navigating a second date, but I do have a few suggestions to help you make the most of it, because – remember – the point of dating is to see whether you like them and whether they're somebody you want to spend more time with. Plus, this gives you another opportunity to see how your personal vibration is affected when you're around them.

Opt for a different setting from the first date. If you went for a coffee or drink on the first date, the second date is a great opportunity to introduce a meal into the picture. There is so much you can find out about someone by dining with them and observing how they speak to waitstaff, how they order, how they feel about food, what their table manners are like, etc. Or perhaps you want to mix it up and go for a bushwalk, to the movies, or to see some live music. Seeing someone in different environments on different dates helps you find out how you feel with them outside the confines of the same venue. It also allows you to see how they shift and change with their environment.

Set an intention for date two. Just as you did for the first date, ask yourself what your intention is for this date. When you can walk into a date clear on why you're there, it gives you more room to relax.

Refer back to things you spoke about on date one. This isn't about going over old ground, but it will show your date that you were engaged and listening to them on the first date. It also gives them an opportunity to ask you how that meeting went or if you ended up catching up with your sister, or whether or not you won that Nobel Peace Prize. This is the sort of thing that builds strong relationships. Good communication!

Dive a little deeper. Small talk is out of the way, so now it's time to dive a little deeper into the stuff that matters to you. You may have enquired into their values, as I suggested you do when getting to know someone on the apps. This is your opportunity to revisit those now that you know them a little better. At this point, I like to find out more about their lifestyle, passions and what they envisage for their future.

Observation is the key to spotting red flags. I mentioned earlier that I seek a partner who has a good relationship with their finances (read: not necessarily lots of finances, just a healthy relationship with them). I won't come right out and ask, 'Hey, how do you feel about money?', but I will notice if they say things like 'I hate money' or 'I could never afford that' or 'I'm so poor.' That kind of language is not aligned with how I'd like to feel with my finances, so comments like that become observational red flags.

Be up front when necessary. As a woman in her mid-thirties, I want to be having babies in the next few years. I don't come out and say, 'Will you have a baby with me?' but I do drop the idea of children into conversation (where appropriate), and I have to say the majority of men I date do the same. A few have come right out and asked me how I feel about having kids. These types of conversations are completely acceptable when you reach a certain age (and even before you do). If this stuff is important to you, you also want it to be important to the person you end up with. If you can find out that it's not on the second date, I say, 'What a relief!' Better than finding out five months deep.

Be honest with yourself. If you raved to all your friends about how great the first date was and you realised on date two that you're just not feeling it, that's okay. I cannot tell you how many second dates I've had where I realised that I just wasn't into them. I honestly believe that when we're not tuned in to our personal vibration we try to make stuff fit on the first date, but more often than not on date two little cracks begin to show. Again, observe this. If you're not sure, definitely go on a third date, or fourth date or fifth until you're certain, but don't force it, or change yourself to make the puzzle piece fit. Trust me, the compression of forcing a square peg into a round hole never leads to a happy relationship.

Post-date feels. Just as you did post first date, ask yourself how you feel after the second date. Are you getting closer or further away from the feelings you want to radiate in a relationship? Is your personal vibration still feeling strengthened around this person? I always question whether or not I felt I was able to be my authentic self or if I felt like I was putting on a bit of a front for them, or holding back, or feeling uncomfortable. You get it.

Dates three, four and five

Experience has taught me that once you make it past that second date, things get a little easier. That's not to say it's all smooth sailing – there's still plenty to be revealed by both parties, I'm sure – but the establishing-a-connection-and-chemistry bit is in full swing.

My advice for these next few dates is much the same as the advice I gave for date two: switch up the setting, dive deeper, be honest, observe those red flags and keep checking back in with how you feel. The whole point of building a kick-ass personal vibration and developing your love GPS is so that you can experience dating as a whole person who knows what they want and what they don't want, and who believes they're worthy and deserving of the person who they attract.

I'm aware that my advice breaks a bunch of dating 'rules' (if you're wondering what rules I'm speaking of, read on). But it's time to change the dating game. If there are things that matter to you, whether it's about the way you express yourself or the things you want in life, what's the point in hiding them? You want to date someone who accepts you exactly as you are. I know that I want to meet the person I end up in a relationship with on the first few dates, not later.

Rules, schmules

In 1995, two American women, Ellen Fein and Sherrie Schneider, came up with a set of 'rules' for dating, which they defined and documented in their book, aptly titled *The Rules: Time-tested secrets for capturing the heart of Mr. Right*. (#vomit) They followed this bestseller with several more books: *The Rules II, The Rules for Marriage, The Rules for Online Dating, All the Rules*, and, more recently, *Not Your Mother's Rules*.

Now I don't want to blow your mind too much, because health and safety should always be a priority, but THERE ARE NO RULES! At least not a set of rules that apply to absolutely everybody. I like to think of myself as a bit of a rebel, but the lessons contained in books such as the aforementioned ones have become such a part of the social and cultural landscape that even if we haven't read the book, we're likely to be following the rules regardless.

A quick peek on Wikipedia reveals 35 of Fein and Schneider's early rules. These are rules invented 25 years ago, sure, but they're worth revisiting because some manage to persist today (I'm not making these up):

- ♥ Don't talk to a man first.
- ♥ Don't call him and rarely return his calls.
- ♥ Don't accept a date for a Saturday night after Wednesday.
- ♥ Stop dating him if he doesn't buy you a romantic gift.
- ♥ Don't see him more than once or twice a week.
- ♥ Don't open up too fast.
- ♥ Be easy to live with.
- ♥ Don't break the rules.

This is just a snapshot of some of the 50-plus rules outlined in their original book, but there are likely a bunch of rules you subconsciously adhere to that aren't in the book. I've discovered that there is actually only one rule that you need to apply when dating and when trying to decide whether or not you should text, call or lean in for a kiss, and it is this:

Check in with your personal vibration at all times.

Let's set up a scenario so I can give you some relatable examples. You've been out on two dates and they both went really well.

You felt a connection and there was serious chemistry. You kissed on the second date and he asked you if you'd be interested in going for a bushwalk next weekend. You gleefully agree, but when Friday rolls around you still haven't heard from him to make a plan. Do you:

a) Text him to say, *Hey, we still on for that bushwalk? Where shall we go?*
b) Do nothing. If he hasn't texted me he mustn't be keen. Let it go.

This is where your personal vibration comes into play. I am a planner and a go-getter. So, although I would feel like I should probably be the submissive and choose option B because society says that's how heterosexual dating works, I know that option A is actually more aligned with my authentic self. And I figure the initiator and planner in me will be the gal he'll eventually end up dating, right? So why hide that side of myself? In this instance I'd ask myself, *How will option A make me feel? And if he doesn't reply to my text is it going to make me feel better or worse than choosing option B?*

It's honestly that simple. Which choice is more aligned with your values? Which choice will make you feel how you desire to feel in a relationship? Which choice will make your vibration feel strengthened? Because here's the thing with rules: it's impossible to apply them to everyone. And while I'm sure a bunch of women nabbed a man hook, line and sinker after reading *The Rules*, I know that if doing that required me to be a submissive, unopinionated and low-maintenance woman who never allowed herself to be vulnerable in order to be in a relationship, then three things would be true. Firstly, that would be the wrong relationship for me; secondly, I'd be fucking miserable; and thirdly, I wouldn't be my authentic self at all, which means my personal vibration would barely be functioning.

If I had to suggest one more thing, not for the sake of restricting you, but rather to keep you level-headed and bring you back to the present moment, it would be this: quit fabricating scenarios in your head.

We've all been there. Perhaps you tried to make sense of the last text he sent – dissecting his every word or creating stories about why you haven't heard from him. But this is not helpful. The best thing you can do is check back in with your personal vibration. Work on strengthening it, and if you hear back from him, wonderful. He probably felt your frequency. If not, also wonderful, he was not in alignment with you and it's time to move on. Because it actually doesn't matter if not hearing back from him means he's just not that into you or not; what matters is that you want someone who you do hear from, right?! Simple.

Dating FAQs (not rules)

I'm not about to talk down 'the rules' then give you a bunch of rules to follow, but I know you're curious about what throwing the rules out might look like. Be warned, though, I'm going to sound like a broken record, because, honestly, it all comes down to how things make YOU feel. So here are some frequent dating questions and dilemmas, along with examples of what I do in these situations. See if these resonate with you.

Who pays?

Honestly, there are no rules here. I always offer to go halves, but if a date insists on paying the entire bill, I let them. And I usually say I'll get the next one (but only because I mean it). If they want to go halves or get the entire bill on the next date, too, again I let them. If they don't offer, then I happily pay as promised. This aligns with my personal values, but it's totally up to you and your own value system. I have some girlfriends who would be appalled at having to pay for a date. I have male friends who feel it's rude for women not to offer. My gay friends say you both have to insist on paying, and it usually gets split. So how could we possibly put down a blanket rule? Determine what feels good for you. If you're the kind of person who likes to feel financially equal in a relationship, the bill dance is the perfect place to set the tone.

Kissing on the first date?

Do you WANT to kiss them on the first date? That's honestly the only question you need to ask yourself. If you're an initiator by nature, I'm not about to tell you to act coy. Kiss them! If they don't kiss you, should you read into it? Nope! They're likely nervous. That's all I have to say on this. If you haven't had a kiss by date three, it might be time to enquire why. But I guarantee that if they're taking you out on a third date, they want to kiss you – they're just deciding how to make their move.

I got four dates deep without a kiss when I was dating Corey. Our first date was a coffee date and a kiss didn't quite feel appropriate. On date two we went for drinks and said our good-byes outside a busy bar with bright streetlights and a long line of people waiting for cabs. We hurriedly hopped into separate cars with nothing but a kiss on the cheek. He picked me up in his car for date three to take me out to dinner, and I was sure it was going to happen that night. I mean, we'd already organised the fourth date while still on the third. But when he dropped me home, there was an awkward goodbye and another cheek kiss and I exited the car feeling deflated, rejected and confused. Corey and I had incredible chemistry, the connection was clear, but the no kiss thing stumped me. He texted me after our date, as he always did. *Thanks for another great night, I'm really enjoying getting to know you, Corey. x* So he's happy to send a kiss via text message but not IRL? I texted back, and decided the up-front approach was the right tactic, and it felt authentic to me. *I had a great night too; the only thing that would have topped it would have been a goodbye kiss.*

I've changed Corey's name, but if I were to give you a blow-by-blow account of our text conversation, I'd probably still be overstepping the privacy mark. The general gist, though, was that he wanted to kiss me, but the right opportunity never came up, and then I hopped out of the car before he got the chance. He said, *I was trying to be respectful, but see now it came across as uninterested.* Well yeah, Corey. It did but ... understood. Our fourth date commenced with a lot of pashing. The end.

I share this story because I often think about how we can read into situations, make assumptions and convince ourselves of things that just aren't true, and how easily we can clear things up with simple communication. So, if you want to lean in for a kiss, do it. If you're waiting for them, wait patiently. If they're taking too long, ask why! Thanks for listening to my TED Talk.

When should you have sex?

There are a few questions I always ask myself when I'm thinking about sleeping with someone, and you might like to do the same: *Do I WANT to have sex with them? What is my intention? How do I feel? How is it going to make me feel tomorrow?* We're going to talk about the energetics of having sex with a partner in chapter 12, but the only person who can know the right time to have sex with someone for the first time is you. Personally, once I have sex with someone something changes for me. And if I haven't established how I feel about them before sleeping with them, I find that the sex can blur my vision a little. I tend to wait until about date four or five before jumping between the sheets. This isn't a rule, I evaluate on a date-by-date basis. Sure, sometimes I've jumped in too early and regretted it. But other times I've probably been more wary than I needed to be. What I've learned is that as long as I keep checking in with my personal vibration, I rarely wake up with regret.

How important are common interests?

I'm controversially going to say not important at all, as long as you have core values and relationship values in common. Whether you both enjoy yoga or abseiling matters very little if you value independence while your partner loves to do all the things together. I actually prefer dating someone who has different interests from mine. It means I have the opportunity to learn about new things and I get to introduce them to a few things that they're likely not familiar with.

Having things in common is less important than someone being accepting of your differences. For example, I'm an introvert, which means I get my energy from being alone and having my space. This is how I recharge my batteries. This does not mean I can't date an extrovert. I actually *love* extroverts, but they need to be conscious of the fact that while they recharge their batteries by being out among people, I am the opposite. As long as we have a mutual understanding of this, it's fine. But if they're the kind of person who needs me to come to every single party with them and takes offence when I'd rather stay in, then the relationship is going to go to shit pretty fast.

Rather than judging your compatibility by your interests, start looking at compatibility more in terms of value alignment, energy input and output, and how that person affects your personal vibration.

When do we make it official?

I'm going to keep this short and sweet. The minute you question your relationship status is the minute you should have the conversation about it. But before you start interrogating them, ask yourself if you're asking from a place of genuinely wanting to explore the relationship or because you're scared of losing them and need your relationship to be defined. If it's the latter, ask yourself what *you* want to feel, and if being around that person enables you to feel those things.

As you've probably gathered, it doesn't matter what dating question you throw at me, I'm going to keep throwing back a variation of the same two things:

1. How do you feel?
2. How is your personal vibration affected?

And honestly, that's it, friends! Everything you need to know about dating. You really are in possession of the ultimate Magic 8-Ball – your own big, bangin' intuition.

Chapter 11

50 ways to leave your lover

We've spent so much of this book gearing up for a higher love. A love that lifts you up, prioritises how you feel and what you value, and, most importantly, a love that strengthens your personal vibration. When it comes to exiting relationships, we want to bring the same level of integrity: a higher exit, if you will.

So, you've landed yourself a hot date, and perhaps that hot date turned into two or three or four hot dates, but now you've realised that you're just not that into them. That is totally your prerogative and you're free to change your mind whenever you like. Part of taking action and dating more IRL is that you're going to date and experience more people. And a consequence of that is that you're not going to vibe with all of these people, and that's okay; it's part of the dating process. That's why another crucial part of dating and taking action is knowing when something isn't quite right, and then doing something about it. With the social phenomenon of ghosting on the rise, it's so important that we learn how to be good humans, keep our personal vibration intact and exit any dating exchanges with dignity, class and respect. Don't be caught doing the digital equivalent of climbing out the bathroom window or feigning an overseas work transfer. Close that loop!

Do you remember that episode of *Sex and the City* where Berger broke up with Carrie via a Post-it Note that read *I'm sorry. I can't. Don't hate me.* It wasn't so much the note itself that was horrendous; it was his inability to show up for an uncomfortable conversation (that FYI, Berger, no one enjoys). It was the lack of respect for what was an actual connection and the lack of common human courtesy that was so deplorable. I find myself thinking of this episode often, having been ghosted several times with incidents ranging from abandoning chat via an app to a successful first date with no follow-up. And then there was that one time when I was actually in a full-fledged relationship and he disappeared like a fart in the wind. I might have preferred a Post-it break-up to that.

What is ghosting?

According to the *Oxford English Dictionary*, ghosting is the act of ending a personal relationship with someone by suddenly and without explanation withdrawing from all communication. As someone who thrives on communication but also, you know, manners, I cannot get my head around just disappearing from a connection, no matter how brief, without so much as a 'Thanks, but no thanks'.

I think that any form of communication deserves closure. I can totally understand chatting with someone on a dating app, not feeling a connection and just never replying. THAT I can deal with. Or perhaps you go out on a date, it's mutually terrible, you both part ways at the end and are not at all surprised when you hear nothing from them again. THAT I can also understand. But that isn't the type of ghosting I'm referring to; I'm talking about situations where a connection has been made and things seem to be going well until one day that person disappears into thin air as if they never existed.

The following scenario has played out for me twice. First date goes exceptionally well. During the date they suggest a second date. At the end of the date, they profess they had a great time and say, 'Speak soon.' Their follow-up text later that day or the next day reads, *So nice to meet you, yadda, yadda, yadda. I look forward to seeing you again*. And then, POOF! They disappear in a puff of smoke! Never to be heard from again.

I have a few questions for the ghosts of this world:

- ♥ Why bother saying you're enjoying the date if you have no intention of seeing me again?
- ♥ Why send a follow-up message after the date to indicate you're keen?
- ♥ What happened? Lose interest? Totally fine, but then say something. I would much rather hear that you're just not feeling it or you got back with your ex, or work is so busy or [insert any legitimate excuse here]. But to just disappear? So weak!

Ghosting isn't uncommon, perhaps you've even done it yourself, but I must let you know that ghosting has everything to do with the person who ghosts and absolutely nothing to do with the one who is ghosted. Nobody (the exception being abusive or offensive folk who just won't take no for an answer) deserves to be ghosted. Disappearing without a trace is one of the most cowardly things a person can do. If you have been ghosted, know that you have dodged a cowardly bullet.

Ghosting is essentially a real-life example of our brains' flight, fight or freeze response. A ghost is a fleer. But rather than fleeing danger to survive, which is the purpose of this response, they flee from confrontation, uncomfortable conversations or, in some cases, the fear of hurting someone's feelings.

Please don't ever be the ghost. In certain situations, like the ones I mentioned on pages 242–3, it can be acceptable, but as soon as you connect in real life, you can't just disappear without a trace. If you aren't concerned for them, then do it for your own energetic alignment. I honestly think the most respectful thing you can do for a person is tell them exactly how you feel (this also applies once you're in a relationship) and at the very least where they stand (perhaps more appropriate when dating), even if that involves an uncomfortable conversation.

If you're looking to beat a hasty (but kind) retreat, here are some scripts you might like to use.

SCENARIO 1
You've been chatting on a dating app or via text
(not fully dating, but more than just a 'hey, how are you')

Thank you for some great chats, but at this stage I don't feel a connection. I wish you all the best.

Simple, honest and respectful.

SCENARIO 2
You've been on a few dates but you're just not feeling the chemistry you had hoped for

It's been a pleasure getting to know you over the last few dates, but I'm looking for someone to develop a deep connection with and I don't believe we're in full alignment. I wish you all the best.

If they bought you dinner, thank them for that. If you'd genuinely like to be friends, suggest it – but only if you mean it. Know that you don't owe them an apology, and you certainly don't need to take the blame for things not working out, so steer clear of 'It's not you, it's me'.

SCENARIO 3
You've been out a few times and had some decent dates. You slept together and you'd hoped that would ignite the fire, but it's not happening.

Sorry, but this one calls for a face-to-face conversation or, at the very least, a phone call. I suggest being honest and not laying any blame on either of you. Something along the lines of:

This isn't heading in the direction I was hoping. I want to be honest with you and let you know that I'm just not feeling how I would like to at this stage. I think it's best if we end things now.

But please, personalise it to your experience...

I guess the best way to look at ghosting is this: if you're the one wanting to ghost, ask yourself how it would make you feel if someone you were chatting with/dating/in a relationship with just disappeared with no explanation?

If you've just been ghosted, take comfort in knowing that a ghost is avoiding any number of things including confrontation and the possibility of hurt feelings, but at the very heart of it they are a coward, and their decision to ghost is a reflection on them, not you.

Don't forget to close that loop

I mentioned closing the loop back in chapter 9 in relation to conversing on apps, but whether you're on an app, dating or in a relationship, energetically that loop must be closed. This is where we often get stuck in the in-between, when a relationship hasn't ended properly and there's a lot of grey area around why something didn't work out.

Sometimes you won't get closure from the other person. In those instances, it's important that you close the loop yourself. If you still have questions, it's okay to ask them, but you need to be okay with either not receiving the answer you want or not getting any response at all.

If you're the person ending the relationship, I truly believe the most respectful thing you can do for a person is tell them how you feel and why you've chosen to end it. That way it's clear and there is no room for misinterpretation.

I messed this up big time with Kurt. The first time I broke up with him, I was a bit of a chicken, and so I blamed a lot of it on myself. I said I wasn't over my last partner, and that he was a great guy but I just wasn't in the right place to be dating. I thought I was doing both of us a favour, but I wasn't. I was lying to myself because the truth was that if I'd met the right guy, I would have been in the perfect place. By telling him he was great when he wasn't and blaming it on my own problems, I gave him fresh impetus to keep pursuing me.

I got it right the second time, after he had decided to kidnap me and drive me across state borders without my permission (sounds like a midday movie plot, but this was very much my real life). That gave me a lot of clear reasons why 'this' wasn't going to work, but regardless of the drama of it all, being clear on why a loop is being closed means you're staying authentic to yourself and giving that other person the information they need to find closure. You don't have to go into the intricate details of why you don't see a future together. The point is not to hurt their feelings but to CLOSE THE LOOP.

I've given you three alternate scripts to use instead of just disappearing, but I'd also like to offer you a few more methods of saying goodbye with kindness, all of which have been inspired by real-life break-ups – mine and other peoples'. That gives you six decent exit strategies to pop in your toolbelt (you didn't really think I was going to give you 50 ways, did you? Simple and straightforward is always best, but that chapter heading was too good to pass up.) Before reading these, please know that I don't condone all of the following methods; some have been added for comedic value. I'll leave that to your discretion.

1. Call them and tell them exactly how you feel and why you're unable to continue to date or be in a relationship with them. White lies are acceptable but avoid them if possible. My number-one rule when ending something with someone is to be respectful to them and stay true to my values. Yeah, it's going to feel uncomfortable, but it gives them proper closure and hopefully it will give you closure, too.

2. Write a letter IF you don't feel like you can tell them directly to their face. Again, be honest, but don't spend the entire letter pointing out their faults. The point is for them to find closure and for you to close the loop.

3. Send a bunch of flowers with a note that says, *It's been a fun few weeks but you're not for me*. This is a true story and when I quizzed the recipient of the flowers, she said she appreciated the straight-shooting approach and gave the guy an A for effort. But she also said that it was confusing and then made her mad AF. Hmm, personally, I don't hate it.

4. Find a woman who is more suited to him, tell him it's not working out but that you've set him up with his perfect match. I mean, if you could pull this off it wouldn't be so terrible, right? A guy I dated once told me the story of his brother who was dating this girl who he really liked but he just wasn't interested in a relationship and so he set her up with his best mate. Last time I checked their social media, they're still dating. See, cute!

5. Move interstate or overseas if you're desperate and leave no forwarding address. My friend Paula did this, but in a really hilarious turn of events the guy she ran away from

was actually transferred to the same city for work and they ended up having dinner. Now they're married!

At the end of the day, honesty is the best policy when it comes to looking out for your personal vibration and theirs. Also, stand firm on your decision. None of this back-and-forth messiness. A clean break is best for both parties. (I say this as a serial returner.) It rarely works out on the second, third or fourth attempt, unless major changes have been made in the areas that caused contention. Things usually don't work out for a reason. Trust that, check back in with your personal vibration post break-up and move forward with your life. I know I've made that sound easy. If there's heartbreak involved, it can be a little trickier. But never fear, I can help with that, too ...

Bouncing back from heartbreak

Maybe you've recently had your heart broken or perhaps you're terrified of the prospect, so you avoid vulnerability and true intimacy, but I want to tell you that heartbreak is actually a gift. It's certainly nothing to be feared. Recovering from heartbreak needn't be the burden and powerless feat that many make it out to be. After my first heartbreak, I avoided dating at all costs, and when I did eventually date again, I did so with my heart locked in an impenetrable steel cage. But this served no one, especially me. You see, if you date with your walls up and wrap your heart in cotton wool to avoid it breaking, you're missing out on the potential and possibilities that emerge with true vulnerability.

Perhaps, like me, you've been under the false assumption that the remedy to your heartbreak rests with the other person, but in fact everything that's needed to heal from heartbreak is within you and your willingness to forgive yourself, love yourself and be patient with yourself. What I now ask myself after dating disappointments and relationship let-downs is, *What do I need to do, think and feel in order to return to a strong personal vibration?* Because in essence that's all it takes. A way for you to figure out how to get back to YOU.

If I can give you one piece of advice about heartbreak it's this: don't avoid it! Avoiding it means missing out on so many incredible experiences that come from your ability to show up fully when dating. Heartbreak will not kill you; if anything, it will make you stronger. I don't regret one heartbreak I've been through (and boy, some of them were doozies) because they taught me so much about myself – what I will and won't settle for, what my values are, where my boundaries lie, and what I really desire love to feel like.

I'm going to use the terms 'heartbroken' and 'heartbreak' throughout this chapter because they have connotations and meanings that you can most likely relate to, but in no way am I suggesting that heartbreak equals a broken heart. Are we clear?

When you are hurt, disappointed, angry, confused or any of the countless other feelings you experience when you allow yourself to open up and show vulnerability in relationships, it can feel as if your heart has been battered, bruised and shattered into a million pieces. I'm not going to take that feeling away from you, because I get it, it feels so very real at the time. But you know that it's physically impossible for your heart to shatter, right? I know it feels like a really obvious point to make, but I think it's important that the distinction is made.

Having experienced 'heartbreak' several times in my life, the kind that renders you unable to think, talk, eat or sleep, I think it's fair to say that even though it felt like my heart would never recover in this lifetime, eventually it did. What felt like irreparable damage eventually healed, and with a little perspective, self-love and the determination to let go, I'm able to say that my heart is completely intact.

I feel you're not sold on the 'heartbreak is great thing' yet. What if I teach you how to navigate heartbreak so that you emerge a whole person. Would that help? Let's give it a go.

My top tips for dealing with heartbreak

Feel everything! Like really feel it. The sooner you feel what's surfacing for you and let it all out, the faster it moves through you. If you suppress or ignore your feelings, they will fester away and manifest in uncomfortable ways throughout your future relationships.

Get curious. Much like the rest of the advice throughout this book, self-enquiry is the key to personal growth. Get curious about why you're feeling so hurt and what you're capable of doing to make yourself feel better, rather than needing someone else to make you feel better. See the distinction?

Write a letter, but whatever you do don't send it. Remember when you were working on your love story and you wrote letters to your ex-lovers? This is also one of the best ways to process your feelings when experiencing symptoms of a broken heart. It allows you to say the things you wanted to say, and frequently exposes feelings you didn't realise you had. And, more often than not, through this process you find a way to forgive them and yourself. But again, please don't send it. The release is in the writing process, and this is *your* process; it actually doesn't have anything to do with the person the letter is addressed to.

Be patient. I'm not going to tell you that time heals all wounds (even though it usually does), or that there are plenty of fish in the sea (even though there are heaps). I'm not even going to tell you that you're better off without them (even though you are) because none of these things feel helpful in the moment, right? But what I will say is that being patient with yourself is key when it comes to dealing with heartbreak. You can't rush through it, and if you're easy on yourself while processing it all, it will be so much easier in the long run. If you push yourself to move on and tell yourself things like *I should be over this by now*, you're moving away from loving yourself, and that's not helping anyone. Allow yourself to feel without wallowing or playing victim, and know that these things take time.

Love yourself despite ... I've said this a few times and I'm going to keep saying it until it's imprinted in your cells. The most beneficial thing you can do for yourself in general, but especially during times of heartbreak, is to love yourself despite the pain, despite the disappointment, despite the way it ended, despite the part you played, despite the reaction you had to their last text, despite the things you chose to ignore, despite the red wine and dark chocolate binge you've been marinating in for the last few weeks. Despite it all! This is when self-love really makes a difference, because when heartbreak makes you feel void of love in the most amplified of ways, showing yourself love despite x, y or z is going to pull you through, this I can guarantee.

Extract the lessons. Every heartbreak has a silver lining. The lessons you take from it and the meaning you give to it will weigh heavily on how you're affected by it. I always look at the end of a relationship as preparation for the higher love I truly want to call in. I think to myself, *Thank goodness I learned the lessons through this relationship so I won't need to learn them in the next one.* With this outlook, there's no regret or failure.

Have the intention to recover. Like most things in this book, having a clear intention is key. And when it comes to heartbreak, you can only wallow in victim mode for so long. You must have the intention to heal and move on. It is the *only* way to get through it, and this means letting go! My longest relationship was five years, but it lasted more like 12 years because neither of us were willing to fully let go. What a freaking shitstorm. My heart broke over and over again for over a decade because I never had the intention of healing. I was holding on to him and the fantasy of our potential. Please don't do that!

Keep working on your personal vibration. I'm not saying that a strong personal vibration will protect you from heartbreak, because it won't, but what it will do is make you braver when you're dating so that you take more risks. And that's essentially what this book is about. Proving to you that you're incredible and literally have the ability to handle anything because you're a whole person who can fulfil their own needs. It also means that when a relationship ends, you can feel hurt and still continue with your life. You can still feel pain and at the same time laugh with friends. You can still grieve and perform well at work. Your relationship has ended, but what makes you, you is still 100 per cent intact.

I began this book by exposing my tender heart to you. When things ended with Jack I felt like my heart had been ripped out of my chest. I've promised you the full story of this relationship and here it is, but what's noteworthy at this point is that it was a surprising heartbreak – one I didn't see coming. Not the ending of the relationship, that was always on the cards, but my reaction to it when it came completely blindsided me. But it was that blindside that ended up being the greatest gift of all.

The story of Jack

Jack and I began our relationship with zero intention of it becoming serious. I had just moved to a new town and we met the day I arrived. There was an instant connection, but it wasn't an 'OMG, where has this man been all my life' type of connection, more of a 'we have the same sense of humour and just spent six hours talking about everything and nothing' kind of connection. But, if I was being completely honest with you (which I am, because: friends), I have to say I really wasn't attracted to him. He was absolutely not my type. He was younger, a little lost – although slowly finding his way – VERY tall, and I thought, at best, he was someone fun to hang out with. And that's what we did.

We hung out, and each time we hung, I had fun, but I kept reiterating to every friend who enquired, 'It's nothing. I'm enjoying myself but it won't go anywhere. There's no future.' Two-and-a-bit weeks into having much fun, many laughs and lots of adventures, we were hit with a curveball. Jack was offered a dream job overseas. I had to confront my own mixed reactions. I was incredibly happy and proud of him, because this was literally a dream job, but I was also a little disappointed. I mean, we were having so much fun. 'What should we do?' he asked. 'They're still figuring out all the paperwork and visas and it could take anywhere between two weeks and six weeks before I leave. It's up to you. Do you want to call it here, or keep hanging out until I go?' Hmm, what a conundrum we were in. I hadn't seen a future in this relationship anyway, so what was a few extra weeks of fun, right? We decided to just keep doing what we were doing. And this is where it got interesting, folks.

Since there was no future in this relationship, I didn't let myself get annoyed by the trivial things that usually aggravate me and have me dismissing people earlier than I should. The fact that Jack was unable to be anywhere on time *ever*, even when he consciously tried his hardest didn't faze me. Neither did the fact that he wasn't the kind of guy I had imagined myself building a life with, having babies with or even just dating long term because he didn't fit the profile of my 'ideal man'. And you know what, I don't reckon I fit his profile of the 'perfect woman' either. Short, opinionated, Gemini (his track record with

Geminis was not good), older than him, not into sports, and I was always super keen to talk about feelings whereas Jack worried he was a sociopath because he struggled to feel emotion (he wasn't).

Neither of us saw a future in this relationship, so neither of us let the little things become points of contention. Instead, we took more risks than we had in past relationships. I allowed myself to be more vulnerable than I usually would because the fear of losing him was taken away – he was already going. I didn't stew over the things that didn't matter and I took extra special care to appreciate the things that did. We went on grand adventures not knowing which one would be our last. Before we knew it, we'd landed ourselves in a pretty fulfilling, happy and dare I say fuss-free relationship. His visa took nine weeks to come through in the end, so what I originally thought would be a farewell to a friend (with a few benefits) of a few weeks turned out to be an impossible goodbye to a three-month relationship that my heart had become waaay more invested in than I ever intended. I believe my parting words to him (a letter he read on the plane as he left Australia) were *I never imagined I would have fallen as hard as I did. Goddamnit, I never intended to fall at all.* And I truly hadn't.

Long-distance was never on the cards for us. We'd only known each other three months, he had no intention of coming home and we were clear from the beginning that it was never going to be anything serious. So when Jack left, that was that – except it wasn't. My heart hurt. I missed him so much and longed for everything that had just been ripped away from me. I hadn't prepared for this pain. I never saw it coming. We stayed in touch through WhatsApp, but a few weeks in, I could no longer handle the polite messages and courteous responses. I wanted to hear how much he missed me. I wanted to know the longing was mutual. I needed to be told I was impossible to live without. But I didn't get any of those things, perhaps because he didn't feel them, or maybe because he didn't know how to express them, or possibly because there was no point in such declarations. No matter the reason, my heart ached and ached and ached. But life still went on. I laughed with friends, my business thrived, I continued to go on adventures, I even started dating other people, although my heart was still tender. And this is where I get to the pointy end of well, my point.

The pain I felt when things ended with Jack hit me hard, for sure. There was this grief that would catch me off-guard and trigger uncontrollable tears at inopportune times – in moments when I was sure I was past him and had moved on. But around those tender times, my life continued, and I always felt like a whole person. This was 100 per cent down to the fact that I'd been working on my personal vibration before I met Jack, while I was with Jack *and* after Jack left. I missed him, for sure, but I never felt a piece of me was missing, and this was (and is) the key to surviving heartbreak.

Lessons in heartbreak (courtesy of Jack)

The fact that I never saw the heartbreak coming was definitely of great benefit to our relationship. If I had predicted it, I probably would never have stayed with Jack after he announced his departure, and I would have missed out on our incredible three-month adventure. This taught me that there can be upsides to a blind-side. I learned a few other valuable lessons, too.

♥ **Take the pressure off!** Without pressure or expectation on our relationship, Jack and I were able to explore a really wonderful time together. I will be taking this lesson into every relationship I have in the future. By not focusing on the things that don't actually matter, like tardiness or his refusal to miss happy hour, we were actually able to connect on the things that *did* matter, like all-night conversations, intellectual stimulation and sharing our quirky senses of humour.

♥ **Be open, be vulnerable and be yourself.** Since there was an expiry date to our relationship, before proper feelings developed, I found myself taking more risks with Jack. I was always myself because I wasn't worried about losing him. This vulnerability allowed our relationship to move to depths neither of us had intended but that I know I would never take back.

♥ **Your personal vibration won't prevent heartbreak, but it will help you survive it.** When the relationship inevitably ended, and I had fallen way deeper than either of us had expected, my heart hurt, but I didn't break. A piece of me didn't hop on that plane with him. Sure, a person I cared for deeply left, but I still remained a whole person, because I arrived in the relationship a whole person with no gaps needing to be filled. Not only that, but I continued to nurture myself and not lose myself while we were dating, and Jack actually strengthened my vibration while I was with him. In a very poetic way, I guess, this helped me recover after he left and even though there was an onslaught of uncomfortable feelings that blindsided me when it ended, I still always felt like me.

💜 **Someone who adds to your personal vibration is always worth the time.** Was Jack the one that got away? I really don't think so. If Jack had stayed, would we have had a long and flourishing relationship? I can't say definitively (I'm not psychic), but my gut says probably not. Do I regret the time we spent together considering I was left heartbroken? Absolutely not! Jack was this incredible gift that allowed me to explore parts of myself that had been buried so deep from past hurts. He exposed me to qualities that I would love to find in a future partner – qualities I had never considered before. My time with Jack highlighted, so profoundly, how I desire to feel in future relationships, and how being myself is the easiest role to play. It also confirmed that there are certain things I will never compromise on again.

I've had much longer relationships than my one with Jack – ones that truthfully left me more heartbroken. However brief, this was the first relationship I've had where I was able to say, 'I will survive', even on nights when it felt like the grief would swallow me whole. Jack flashed into and out of my life in such a significant fashion that sometimes I wonder what the point was. But one week after he left, I sat down to write this book, and the insight into myself that I had gained through our three short months together have honestly shaped much of what you're reading. So cheers to Jack, but, most importantly, cheers to the power of a strong personal vibration.

Heartbreak myth busters

Now that we've agreed that heartbreak needn't be avoided, there are many myths about heartbreak that I reckon slow down the recovery process, so let's debunk them, shall we?

It takes half the length of time you were with someone to get over them. What a load of bullshit! We humans love applying numbers and timelines to everything. It makes us feel safe, but this formula is based on nothing! A study published in the *Journal of Positive Psychology* says it takes 11 weeks to feel more positive after a break-up, which perhaps holds a little weight, but I just don't think you can put an accurate time on something that is so personal. The healing process will take however long it needs to. What's most important is that you nurture yourself, have the intention to heal and move on.

If you weren't officially dating then it shouldn't hurt as much. First of all, however you feel is valid whether your relationship was 'official' or not, but it's worth putting into perspective where your feelings are coming from. Sometimes, what hurts the most is the fantasy of what could have been. There is a mourning of potential and a feeling of loss, but it's not based on reality. So, ask yourself, *What do I feel is missing and how can I fulfil it within myself?* (Broken record alert.)

A rebound relationship will make you feel better. There's a fine line between dating too soon and not dating soon enough, but finding a person to make you feel all the things you were craving to feel from the recently departed is not the answer. You need to satisfy these things within yourself before jumping to the next person or you'll find yourself in exactly the same predicament. Don't date in the hope that it will erase the feelings you no longer wish to feel or aren't willing to process. It's not going to serve you at all, but also, it's not fair on the other person.

Eventually, you'll feel closure. I think one of the biggest mistakes I've made in past relationships is waiting to feel adequate closure after it has ended. Looking for closure can leave you hanging on for eternity. You need to be okay to move on without closure. Instead, find closure within yourself.

Talking about it will help. Initially yes, but then it's up to you to process your feelings. If you go over and over and over it again with anyone who'll listen, you'll a) drive yourself crazy, b) most definitely drive them crazy, and c) keep perpetuating the story and stay stuck in its narrative.

You can stay friends with someone who broke your heart. I'm friends with only one of my ex-boyfriends. That's not to say there is animosity between me and my other exes, they all still watch my Instagram stories (does that make us friends?), but I definitely don't text them on their birthdays or catch up for impromptu dinners. However, just because I cut ties with all ex-lovers doesn't mean you should. I have plenty of friends who are friends with their exes, but it does come with complications, and it's definitely not authentically achievable until you have healed from the relationship. If you're honest with yourself, you're likely staying friends with an ex because there's a part of you still hanging on to some form of hope. If you can confidently say that you've found adequate closure and see them purely platonically, then all power to you!

Look, I guess what I want you to take away from this chapter is this: heartbreak is definitely a risk when dating, but without taking the risk, you're potentially missing out on a higher love. If you want to be authentic and be yourself in your next relationship, flaws and all, it takes a certain level of vulnerability. *This* is where authentic connection comes from. Remember that a love lost and a tender heart means only one thing: you haven't found your person yet and that potential is now one step closer. I find so much comfort in this. I hope you do, too.

- Chapter 12 -

The energetics of dating

Certain experiences in dating are hard to put into words; repeated patterns play out (as we discovered when looking at our old love stories), we encounter crossroads when met with compromise (sometimes it's not as easy as just aligning your values) and often, our own self-worth issues block us from truly connecting with a potential partner.

After doing a lot of self-evaluation, self-reflection and self-development, I've realised that if you can look at the energy behind why you behave the way you do, or why you accept the way someone else behaves, rather than the act itself, things start to make a lot more sense.

I think you're ready to look at dating from this angle. You're so in tune with your personal vibration now that you'll be able to feel when it's impacted much more rapidly than you could previously. There is so much power in that!

I spoke with energetic healer, kinesiologist and conscious conception doula Zoe Bosco to ask her to break down what goes on from an energetic perspective when it comes to some of the most common relationship and dating dilemmas. I found that once I was able to identify the energetics of the situation, I could quit repeating the same old patterns. Let's dissect eight of these patterns to find out what's really going on.

1. The chase

I've already fessed up to my penchant for 'the chase'. Being chased, chasing others, it doesn't much matter. The thrill of having to make someone earn my love or equally desiring to earn the love of another has an effect on me that a rational mind can't make sense of. If we start to look at it from an energetic perspective, however, things become a little clearer.

This game is a throwback to our primal instincts of predator and prey. Essentially, this dance of survival has somehow been disguised as a romantic pursuit. Bosco explains that 'the chase is a game, much like what we played as kids, except that as children we have no filters, there is no fear of rejection and the risks are low'.

As adults, the risks are much higher. The innocence of the game now has a shadow element to it, and the chase will often play out because you can't express what you want or desire. You see, the chase is a game with no winners; one person is being put on a pedestal at the expense of the other person's feelings of inferiority. 'You could look at the chase as a symptom of not being in full alignment with a partner; a true vibrational match doesn't need to chase or be chased,' says Bosco.

The trap I was stuck in for so long was that if I chased someone and caught them, I felt validated (temporarily). If

THE ENERGETICS OF DATING

I was *being* chased, I thought it meant I was worthy enough to be pursued. But anyone who has been caught in the chase cycle playing either the role of predator or prey knows that the reward is never as rewarding as the pursuit itself.

Bottom line: A person with a strong vibrational frequency and an acute sense of self-awareness does not need the chase. When you're a strong vibrational match for someone, there is a clear energetic alignment, and the worthiness of each individual is validated within themselves, making the partnership all the more rewarding.

Truth bomb: The chase is a reflection of your innate worth and a need to be defined by something outside of yourself. It is the ultimate external validation loop and, as you learned in chapter 3, looking outside of yourself to validate your worth is futile.

2. Unrequited Love

Have you ever loved someone so deeply, so fiercely, so uncondi-tionally, but that love has just not been reciprocated? I've experienced varying degrees of loving someone more than they love me in most of my relationships, and in the relationships where I've loved them less, I haven't tended to stick around for long (yawn). But unrequited love goes deeper than that. Energetically, it's about remaining trapped in a cycle of 'one day they will love me if I do this or say that or love them more'. But according to Bosco, we love someone in all the ways we are crying out to be loved ourselves: 'When it comes to unrequited love, all of your love is being poured into the other person in an attempt for them to love you back, and none of that love is being poured into yourself where it is needed more than ever.'

Again, it comes back to self-worth. When you starve yourself of love, you overcompensate for the malnourishment by loving someone else more – hoping they'll return the love you've deprived yourself of. This is the energy of unrequited love. It isn't grounded in reality; instead, its foundation is built on distorted beliefs and fantasies of what could be.

Bottom line: When you're in vibrational alignment with your partner unrequited love cannot exist. There will of course be ebbs and flows with varying degrees of love as a relationship progresses, but if you work on strengthening your personal vibration and loving yourself first before pouring all of your love into another, you will be pouring your love into fertile ground and giving that love an opportunity to grow.

Truth bomb: Unrequited love is not love, it's a mirror to the love you crave for yourself.

3. Hanging on vs letting go

Have you ever wanted something (or someone) to work so badly that you hang on for dear life, scared of what will happen if you let go? Perhaps a relationship isn't working and you refuse to walk away, or a dating experience isn't progressing how you envisaged but you hang on to the potential of what it could be out of fear of the reality. Hanging on is an energetic trap I've been caught in too many times to count.

I don't give up on things easily. When it comes to learning the recorder or climbing Everest, this is a wonderful attribute, but when it's time to let go of a relationship, I find it a little harder. Bosco shed some light on what happens energetically to love when we hang on for dear life (or, as Aussies like to say, 'flog a dead horse'). 'Love can't breathe to continually grow and evolve with us when we cling on to it, scared of what would happen if we loosen our grip,' says Bosco. 'We hold on out of fear, and by doing so, we limit its expression and its potential to grow into what it's meant to be.'

I know that for me, letting go feels like giving up, but Bosco assures me it's quite the opposite when it comes to love, 'If you're not willing to let something die, you're not giving yourself full permission to live.'

Bottom line: We hold on to love because we're scared to lose it. If you're able to trust and hold faith that what is meant for you will come to you, then there is no need to grip it so tightly.

Truth bomb: If you let go of 'the one' and they don't return, they're not the one that got away, they were simply never 'the one'.

4. Desperate energy

I have been on both sides of desperate energy. In my younger years, desperation arose when I found myself stuck in the afore-mentioned cycle of hanging on and refusing to let go. And more recently I was at the receiving end of desperation from a partner who was so afraid of losing me that he suffocated me with his availability, refusal to ever disagree, and blatant disregard for my personal space. I have never felt more repulsed and repelled in my life.

Bosco explains the energy of desperation by using the three attachment cords of craving, clinging and aversion:

> If someone is desperate, they are void of faith and they attach through craving and clinging, which automatically triggers the polarity of aversion in the person on the receiving end. Desperate energy manifests when someone is seeking something outside of themselves to fulfil and validate either them or the person on the receiving end. Therefore, the answer to diluting desperation is to satisfy within yourself what you're so desperate for in another.

We see this play out so often in the early stages of dating. When someone comes on too strong too soon, it's such a turn-off! It is a leaking of energy that automatically swings us to the opposing emotion of aversion to balance the energy out. Can you observe this within yourself?

Those gaping holes I keep referring to that we seek to have others fill can only be filled by us. When we desperately seek the remedy in another, we actually trigger the opposite reaction in them and push them away.

Remember the Law of Vibration, which states that everything in the universe vibrates on its own frequency, and that things with a similar frequency are drawn together? Well, that similar frequency isn't always the exact replica; sometimes it's the polarity. Think about two puzzle pieces; if they were exactly the same, they wouldn't fit together. Energy works in the same way. If you sit at one extreme of craving and clinging (i.e. desperation), you're going to attract the polarity of that energy to you, which is aversion. Make sense?

Bottom line: If your energy is out of alignment and swinging to an extreme, you're likely to attract the polarity of that energy rather than the equal of that energy. Ask yourself, *What is it that I'm desperately seeking in another and am I able to fulfil it within myself?*

Truth bomb: Desperation equals separation from self.

5. Alone vs loneliness

I've never had an issue being on my own. I've probably remained single longer than I intended at times because I hardly ever find myself lonely. Alone? Sure! I live on my own, and when it's just me, I do fit the dictionary definition of having no one else present. But lonely? Rarely.

Energetically, loneliness and being alone are very different things, even though they often appear to be the same thing. Bosco says, 'Loneliness comes from the distortion of what being alone means.'

We fear being alone because we believe something is missing. Much like desperation, unrequited love and the energy behind the chase, it is this constant search for external validation that breeds loneliness. Ask yourself: *What do I feel is missing when it is just me, and how can I fulfil that within myself?*

Because here is the thing about loneliness: it's not reserved for those who are alone. You can absolutely feel it when you're in a relationship with someone. In fact, I reckon the loneliest I've ever felt is in a relationship where my needs were not being met by my partner and, even more importantly, where my needs were not being met by myself. Bosco says,

> There is this sweet spot when a relationship ends where we have an opportunity to experience the sacred recalibration time of being alone. This time is pure and sacred. It only transforms into loneliness when we project distorted stories onto it. The ending of a relationship is our opportunity to integrate all of the lessons we learned and discover who we are outside of the relationship. However, all too often we'll jump straight into the next relationship because it validates something within us and distracts us from ourselves.

I don't jump from one partner to the next, but I used to. Each time a relationship ended, I'd walk away with big gaping holes all over me, and often they were the same holes I'd walked in with. I'd have to ask myself, *Who am I now?* My identity was so wrapped up in who I was with, that without them I felt incomplete, empty, lost. THIS is why the majority of this book teaches you how to feel like a whole person who can walk into and out of relationships that aren't working because you're not worried about who you'll be without them. And this is what will ultimately save you from loneliness. According to Bosco,

Walking into the dating scene lonely is very different energetically from walking into the dating scene after a period of being alone. Loneliness will fuel the hunt for external validation and somebody to fill all of the gaps, and soon enough you'll find that loneliness follows you wherever you go, alone or not. But, if you can take the opportunity of being alone to practise self-awareness and to strengthen your vibration, then the foundations of the relationship will set you up for a much more rewarding experience.

Bottom line: If you're lonely, it's because you have a distorted view of what being alone is. Ask yourself, *What is missing and how can I satisfy this within myself?*

Truth bomb: Loneliness does not prey on those who are alone. If you don't address its causes, it will follow you wherever you go.

6. Self-love

'How much more do I have to love myself?' I've yelled this in frustration many times. I've already told you that loving yourself is not a prerequisite for receiving love. However, Bosco explains that while it's not always about loving yourself more, there is value in loving yourself in the moments when you find it the hardest. She says, 'The point is not to love yourself more, but to practise loving yourself in the moments when it's most required. How much you've developed the practice of self-love, especially when it's the hardest, reflects how you can show up and love your partner in the moments when it's the hardest to love them.'

Bottom line: The prerequisite for love is not to love yourself more. However, if you want a higher love and to be in full alignment with the love you crave, then you need to be able to love yourself the way you wish to give and receive love. Plain and simple.

Truth bomb: It's not about loving yourself more, it's about loving yourself despite x, y and z. That is self-love.

7. How much baggage is too much baggage?

As we get older and our relationship tally increases, it's an unfortunate reality that we acquire baggage. While we have the capacity to lighten our own load and process the baggage we bring into a relationship, how do we deal with the baggage that another person rocks up with?

Bosco approaches baggage from a really simple standpoint: 'No bag is too big or too heavy if the holder of the bag is holding it themselves! But if they're trying to hide the bag, ignore the bag, make excuses for the bag or ask you to hold the bag for them, then that's when baggage becomes an issue.'

Whoa! Mind explosion. It really is that simple, right? And the same goes for your baggage. If you're willing to take responsibility for the stuff you bring into a relationship, whether that be kids, an illness, an ex-lover or your old tired love stories, then it should never feel like a burden on the other person.

Bottom line: Don't write someone off for the baggage they've acquired before meeting you if they're willing to own it, carry it and take full responsibility for it. Baggage only becomes a problem when it becomes yours to hold.

Truth bomb: Bring all the bags you like, just don't make me carry them!

8. Let's talk about sex

I stuck sex in this chapter because I think looking at it from an energetic perspective is the most beneficial way for you to make your own informed choices about when to have sex, why you're having sex and who to have sex with. I can't tell you whether or not to have sex on the first date, but I can ask you what your intention is, and if you're going to feel fulfilled after doing so. If your answer is yes, go for it! If you're not sure, it's time to check in with your personal vibration.

One might argue that sex changes everything, and I tend to agree. I know for me, once I have sex with someone, I've crossed a line that I find difficult to step back from. My tendencies to 'hang on' amplify, and I often find myself energetically hooked in ways that last longer than the sweet release of oxytocin.

Bosco lays out four centres through which we connect:

1. **Intellect centre.** This is our intellectual connection. It includes communication – conversation, wit and banter.

2. **Heart centre.** This is our connection through love and acceptance. It often manifests through our heartfelt desires and our willingness to open up to love another.

3. **Gut centre.** This is our intuitive knowing and unexplainable connection to someone. This is often described as that feeling of the familiar, a sense of just 'knowing'. That feeling of being pulled towards something without reason or logic.

4. **Physical centre.** This is our physical and primal connection. That feeling where our primal and animal instincts take over.

In the early stages of dating it's likely that you're connecting on the physical (aka sex) centre alone, and while there is absolutely nothing wrong with this, what's important is the awareness that in a long-term relationship this is not a sustainable connection.

At any one time we can be connecting with any combination of these centres, but if you're seeking a higher love and to be relating consciously and fully with your partner, then it's worth attempting to connect on all four centres.

Bosco highlights the importance of intention when choosing to have sex with a partner: 'Connection from any of the four centres is fine as long as it is a mutual intention.'

I've had great sex in terrible relationships and, in retrospect, I can see that this was a purely physical connection. I've had wonderful heartfelt and intellectual connections with a partner and mediocre physical connection, and honestly, it's not necessarily a recipe for a better relationship. However, can you see how spending time developing an emotional and intellectual connection before exploring the physical connection can lead to a much more connected experience?

THE ENERGETICS OF DATING

Bosco explains 'Unfortunately in [heterosexual] dating, women especially can bypass the intellect, heart and gut centres to meet the primal surge that comes from the sex centre, because we think it's expected of us. Often this will be imprinted from sex at an early age, when we develop the belief that having sex is how you keep a partner, how you satisfy them, and if you don't do it, someone else will.'

I have absolutely fallen into this trap, and I am a smart and emotionally intelligent woman. However, without taking the time to develop a connection that goes past the physical, I have been known to find myself in a dysfunctional sexual relationship.

Perhaps you can relate to the following thought patterns: *Why am I doing this?* (Intellect) *I don't even really like them!* (Heart) *I know I shouldn't be doing this* (gut), *but at the same time it feels so good* (physical).

Bosco makes an important distinction: 'Dysfunction only occurs when both parties are not aware of the intention. It's okay to have a purely primal connection if you're in alignment with your partner's desire, but if you're connecting through the heart and they're connecting through the physical, then this is where things get muddy.'

Having an emotional connection with your partner before sex is not always necessary if your intention is just to have hot sex. However, what you might like to consider before jumping into bed with someone for a mindless, emotion-free romp is how strong your emotional connection to self is, because this can make things messy.

Do you know what you need in order to feel safe? Do you know what your terms of consent are? Before I sat down to write this chapter, I had never considered what my values and boundaries were when it came to sex. (How wild is that?) But as important as your core values and love values are when it comes to your personal vibration, it's also helpful to at least have an idea of where your limits lie when it comes to sex. This doesn't mean that you can't be fluid or that you're bound by what you once gave consent to, but it enables you to align to what's true for you in the moment so that you don't override a certain part of yourself.

Bosco says, 'If you're giving your body over without the consent of your heart, you're essentially abandoning self. It's important to undertake an inner enquiry and to know your boundaries so that you can feel safe to open up to sex (on all four centres). If you're not in integrity with your centres, you're unable to open up to the divinity of sex.'

Another thing to contemplate when considering doing the 'deed' with a new partner is the exchange of energy that is taking place. Bosco explains, 'We're energetic beings, made up of energy, and when we have an intimate experience with a partner, there is an exchange taking place. Your energy imprints on them and theirs on you.'

Now *this* is worth contemplating. When you date someone, you're already having an energetic exchange with them. Your vibrations are trying to align with their vibrations, you're looking to feel a heartfelt connection, an intellectual connection and, sure, that gut feeling would be great, too. But when you have sex with someone, you're literally exchanging energy with them (and not just through your bodily fluids). Bits of your energetic make-up are embedding in their vibrational field. Now I'm not going to go as far as to say watch out for energetic STDs, but I tell you, if I had been aware of this energetic exchange with some of my previous partners, I would not have had sex with them.

So when the hell do we have sex when dating? Do you have to wait until you're connected on all four centres? Must you contemplate forever walking around with bits of every sexual partner's energy imprinted in your cells? God, no! Imagine!

Again, this is a personal preference that I encourage you to integrate into your personal vibration. When contemplating sleeping with someone, ask yourself these questions:

- ♥ *What is my intention behind wanting to have sex? Am I trying to validate something within myself? Am I trying to prove something to myself or someone else?*
- ♥ *What are my sexual values and boundaries?* After much contemplation, I decided that as long as I feel safe, connected and clear about my intentions, then it's easier to say yes or no at any moment throughout the experience.
- ♥ *Which centres are my priority?* For me, it's all four. I've tried all the different variables and have to say that they all hold equal weight. They may not for you, and that's okay. – as long as you're clear from the get-go what's important to you and you ensure that your partner's desires are in agreement with those.

Bottom line: Your intention behind sex will determine its impact on you and your relationship. If you can mutually connect on all four centres with your partner, you'll likely be able to create a strong foundation for a sexual relationship.

Truth bomb: Who you choose to have sex with impacts you energetically. Choose wisely.

You've most likely cottoned on to the recurring theme throughout each of the aforementioned energetic scenarios: when you're out of energetic alignment with yourself (doing things like running old love stories, not taking responsibility for your own stuff, seeking external validation from others and ignoring your own ability to love yourself fully), your energy will begin to leak all over the goddamn place. Two simple questions to ask yourself are: *What do I need right now?* And *Can I satisfy this within myself?* The answer to those two questions is the answer to all of the above.

As you progress through the dating experience, whenever you feel shifts of energy bringing you out of alignment, stop. Take a deep breath. Ask yourself, *What am I feeling? Why am I feeling this?* And finally, *How can I make myself feel the way I desire?* Your feelings are data and information. They create an energetic frequency that determines how a situation will unfold, and the only person responsible for your energy is YOU.

You've also got a superpower – your personal vibration. You're so aware of what it feels like when you're in alignment now, that you'll feel even the slightest shift in it. Use this as your radar. It will indicate where you need to address your own insecurities and worth, and will also help you identify where others are leaking their energy. This gives you the opportunity to say, 'Not today,' and walk away with your energy and heart intact.

- Chapter 13 -

Love-related
aha moments

We're nearing the final pages of this book, which means that it's nearly complete – unlike you, who will never be complete because you're ever-evolving. And by now you know that you don't need someone to complete you because you're already whole – unlike this book, which needs me to finish writing it.

I feel confident that as we begin the penultimate chapter of this book, you're at the very (very) least open to dating. Hopefully, you're already actively dating and you feel confident about finding a vibrational match because you're so tuned in to your own personal vibration. And, if I've done my job correctly, you should also feel well equipped to create a higher love that makes you feel less like you're falling and more like you're rising in love. Gold stars for all of us!

Since we've touched on break-ups and heartbreak, I didn't feel it appropriate to end this book about dating and finding love without passing on some sage advice about relationships. After all, that's hopefully where all of these dates are leading.

And while I've dropped little nuggets about this throughout this book, I thought it might be nice to dedicate an entire chapter to some of the aha moments that I've had about love that completely changed not only the dating game for me but also the way I experience love, give love and, most importantly, receive it.

Please know that all of the advice below is based on my personal experience. Some of it may resonate with you, some may not. Take it or leave it (but please do take most of it – a lot of blood, sweat and tears were poured into learning these lessons).

Love advice from me (and John Legend) to you

The following is a series of lightbulb moments I've experienced while dating, loving and being in relationships. There are truth bombs, love bombs and a few 'is-she-serious' bombs – and some are going to be a little harder to take than others. But I learned all of the following lessons the hard way, so hopefully you won't need to. You're welcome.

I've also included a few pieces of love advice from some favourite love songs, 'few' being the operative word. My research assistant Laura and I dived deep into songs, both recent and old, in search of some sage love advice to share in a light and enjoyable manner because we're fun like that. But to our shock (or maybe not), we found it very hard to find songs that weren't laced in tragedy, heartbreak or messed-up circumstances (refer back to chapter 6 for more context). After hours of falling into the black abyss of our music library, we managed to conjure up a few great pieces of advice for you. But FYI, it might be a good time to stop thinking your favourite love songs are shining examples of the love you want to create in your life.

Does this love have legs? Love isn't always easy (don't let any rom-com convince you otherwise) but it should never feel like a constant effort to make it work. If it's hard work and you struggle to feel strong in your personal vibration, it might be love but it's not a sustainable love, and it's definitely not a higher love.

Stay present. It's so easy to project yourself into a future that has yet to be created with a partner you've just started dating, but I urge you to stay in the present moment as much as possible. Enjoy each day and the experience you're having right now rather than worrying about whose house you're going to move into, how many guests you'll have at the wedding or whether or not you'll have joint burial plots.

Take the pressure off. When you date people just for the fun of dating them, rather than interview them for the position of your life partner, not only do you find out things about them that you may have otherwise dismissed prematurely, but it also gives them an opportunity to reveal themselves organically.

Ignore Beyoncé (well, don't do that, I mean just that one song). Healthy in love, calmly in love, sanely in love is always more rewarding than CRAZY in love. Are we clear?

Don't dismiss people too soon. If you feel something on the first date, but things didn't quite go to plan, give it another opportunity. But in the same vein, if you feel like something isn't quite right, don't force it. Listen to your gut.

Actions speak louder than love songs. John Legend, 'Actions', 2020. This took me years to figure out. Replace love songs with promises, excuses, and 'but I love yous', and you have my dating life up until a few years ago. Words are my jam, but if your partner is not showing you love through their actions and proving that they are 'active' in your relationship, then you're not actually dating or relating to them, you're having a relationship with their vocabulary.

Vulnerability really is the key to intimate relationships. I learned this the hard way, by seeing vulnerability as a weakness. But here's the thing that saved me: my personal vibration. You see, with a strong personal vibration you can be as vulnerable as you like because whatever happens when you open yourself up, you can always bounce back. ALWAYS.

Stop questioning why they're not taken. Have you ever met a great guy and then thought to yourself, *Why the hell is this guy still single? What's wrong with him?* First of all, remind yourself that you're still single and you're fantastic, and then simply say, 'Thanks for waiting for me.'

Complicated is an Avril Lavigne song, not a relationship status. Relationships should make life easier, more rewarding and brighter. If your relationship is making life more complicated, it's time to reassess.

Don't date someone's potential. Sure, give them an opportunity to reveal themselves to you, but if you're chasing the person you desire them to be rather than who they are right now, you're not actually in a relationship with them. I've spent my whole life dating the potential of partners. Trust me, it's a futile pursuit for you and it's not fair for them either.

Your worth is yours for validating. Don't ever let your hope, worth or validation rest in the hands of someone else's unwillingness to choose you, propensity to change you or inability to show up for you. Your relationship should be based on who you are now. If they can't accept that, move on.

Don't ever be afraid to love. Love is big, love is bold, but love will not break you if you enter with a strong personal vibration.

Don't go changing, to try and please me. Billy Joel, 'Just the Way You Are', 1977. This whole book has been making you feel like a whole person, so don't go changing yourself to please someone else. This is also true for the way you show love. If someone doesn't like your affection or your words, then they're not aligned with the way you give and receive love. Find someone who is.

THIS: Don't ever fight for someone who wouldn't fight for you. When you say no to people who don't show up for you, you're strengthening your personal vibration and raising your self-worth.

Speak your truth. Don't ever be scared to say, 'I love you', 'I miss you' or 'I'm sorry'. All powerful. All honest. All worthy of speaking and being heard. If your words are not received well, at least you can say you were honest with yourself.

Weather the storms together. Ever been trapped between two flooded bridges with your partner and been forced to take refuge in a stranger's house for five days while suffering from pneumonia? *Putting my hand up over here* No, but seriously, disasters, illness, family deaths or any kind of big life events that force us into survival mode are clear indicators of how a person shows up in a relationship and how you can effectively communicate with and comfort each other.

You've got to learn to leave the table when love is no longer being served. Nina Simone, 'You've Got to Learn', 1965. A relationship is often over long before it ends, and while there is merit (sometimes) in sticking around to make things work, if you're not receiving the love you need in a relationship, it's okay to walk away.

Closing one door will open another. The longer you lament a love that was lost, the longer you prevent the next opportunity from coming in. Close the loop. Feel the feelings. Forgive. Get back to strengthening that personal vibration.

You can't make your heart feel somethin' it won't. Bonnie Raitt, 'I Can't Make You Love Me', 1991. I've dated a lot of really great guys I just didn't feel anything for. Forcing it didn't work and was also incredibly unfair on them. I would be so offended if someone had to force themselves to feel something for me.

Unrequited love is not love. If someone tells you that they don't love you (or shows you that they don't love you), don't make it your life's mission to change their mind. Instead, take your love for them and turn it back on yourself, a much more worthy recipient.

Nothing sucks joy out of you faster than waiting for a phone to buzz. When you wait by the phone for a text or a call or an Instagram story view, you're passing your worth over to the other person. Put the phone down and do something that brings you joy instead.

Make this one into a bumper sticker: Rejection is your cue to accept yourself more.

Don't create a PowerPoint presentation of why you should be together. Convincing someone you're perfect for them is a sure-fire way to weaken your vibration. I spent the better part of 12 years trying to convince an ex he'd passed up 'the one'. I did everything short of presenting a TED Talk in his honour. What I should have been doing is finding the person who didn't need to be convinced.

Sometimes, love is where you least expect it. I cannot stress this enough. You can't predict how you're going to meet someone, so quit walking around with preconceived ideas that might be potentially blocking someone incredible from coming into your life.

Don't try to change other people. Change your hair, change your clothes, change your underwear (please, change your underwear), but don't ever try to change someone else to fit your expectations.

Admit when you're wrong – it's a superpower. When you can admit that you're wrong, you become the strongest person in the room.

Love advice from the experts

I reached out to the following experts, who look at love and relationships in a way that's outside your basic psychology textbook, in order to get to the heart of love advice that can be felt deeply and practised by everyone.

'So often, I witness relationships end not because there is a lack of love, but from lack of good communication. Truths left unspoken, hearts not shared and feelings withheld will suck the life right out of a relationship. So, **in order to have epic relationships, we need to get really good at communication and expressing our needs, fears and desires.** It goes a long way to ensuring each partner feels valued, seen, acknowledged and respected.'

Tara O – Sex and relationship coach

'Romantic relationships can be challenging, there are simply no two ways about it. **My advice is to dedicate your resources such as time, energy and money to knowing yourself.** Know yourself so well that every area of your life (including romance) is a meaningful expression of a part of you.'

Debbie Zita – Leadership and relationship strategist for Inspired Women

'**You do not have to wait to be chosen by love before you can experience the fullness and depth of love. Love is within you, alive and vibrant in every moment.** The moment you recognise, acknowledge, feel and embrace the love beating within your own heart, is the moment you are in direct alignment with love. Savour and relish in those moments, bathe in them, cultivate them and expand them. Choose love first and then it will be reflected in miraculous and beautiful ways around you, sometimes in ways you least expect. Be open to love, choose love, trust love is with you.'

Zoe Bosco – Kinesiologist, energy worker and conscious conception doula

'**The more you can learn about, sit within and enjoy your own nature (this includes your values, wants and needs), the better positioned you will be to draw in a partner who is compatible with you.** Astrology readings between couples show that we are both teacher and student to each other: in some areas we provide friction while in others a soothing balm, and when we are triggered there is learning to be had – you can either react or reflect. The healthiest couples that I read for have gone through the process of becoming aware of their own patterning and unconscious behaviours, meaning that they are less likely to repeat unhealthy relationship patterns. One tidbit, if you are constantly attracting one type of Sun or Moon sign or a particular archetype into your life, get digging. Learn all you can about that sign/archetype and do the work within yourself to see why this character keeps showing up – it's not chance.'

Jules Ferrari – Psychological astrologer

Love advice from everyday peeps

I also asked a bunch of strangers for their most valuable piece of love advice. Here is what they shared.

'Don't let your expectations let you down. When you're upset and feel let down by your partner, first ask yourself if their only misdemeanour was failing to meet expectations set by you.' – WOAH. This is great and so very true!

'Make sure you actually like the person you're with. Dating is your opportunity to ask yourself: Do I actually like this person or is it just physical attraction?' – I have been 'crazy' in love with a bunch of guys that it turns out I didn't even really like. Like can grow into love.

'Be a team player.' – You're in a relationship. You should be able to come together as a team. There's no 'I' in team, folks!

'Find intimacy in small moments. This is the key to a sustainable long-term relationship.' – Yes! Intimacy can be taken for granted, especially when it loses the passion of those early stages of dating and life gets busy. Can you consciously introduce intimacy into even the tiniest moments?

'Love is the easy part. It makes the hard parts of the relationship worth it.' – Nuff said!

'Never go to bed angry.' – This is a great one, but I'm also of the opinion that sometimes a disagreement needs a little room to breathe, and a good night's sleep can provide a new perspective. Navigate this one on a case-by-case basis.

'Compromise is key.' – It'll save your relationship as long as you're not compromising on your core values and authenticity.

At the end of the day, I truly think the best piece of advice always comes from your own innate wisdom and your ability to tune in to your personal vibration. It will always be the authority on whether a relationship is working or not. It's then up to you to listen, to follow the niggles and to honour your own frequency, knowing that doing so not only strengthens your vibration but also makes you a magnet for more of what is in alignment with you (aka a higher love).

All love stories get a happy ending, right?

I'm going to be up-front with you. When I initially mapped out the contents of this book, I had a clear plan in place. I'd kick things off by teaching the importance of a personal vibration and how, when strengthened, it becomes your number-one superpower. Next, I'd introduce the concept of love vibrations, discuss how we've messed them up and demonstrate how, if we simplify love, we actually end up with a really pure vibrational essence. Then I'd have some fun by teaching you all of the valuable lessons I've learned about dating. We'd explore the ways you can date differently so that it becomes a rewarding experience rather than a painful one.

I planned to share lots of my own personal stories, throw in a bunch of real-life stories of regular people, interview some experts and, ya know, eloquently expand the microcosm of what it means to date and find that higher love. Simple! Then, my big plan was to finish it all up with an epic happy ending. And not just a sweet last chapter that leaves you satisfied with the commitment you've given to reading an entire book, but a full-blown romantic, heart-exploding love story, the kind you would be happy forking out the cost of a large popcorn for, because, well, what better way to prove the power of my prose?

As is often the case with most creatives, I live the work I am currently writing. I believe the French would call me *un cobaye*; in English, a guinea pig. In the same way a method actor completely emotionally identifies with the part they're portraying, I (not always intentionally) live out the teachings as I pen them. This is perhaps where my false sense of certainty came from. My brain told me, *Do the work you believe in so deeply, finish writing the book you know will change lives and as a result the happy ending everyone's been holding out for will be delivered to you on a silver platter.*

But what exactly are the prerequisites of a happy ending? The 'classic' Hollywood-style happy ending conveniently ceases at the point the cameras stop rolling, when the characters no longer have a narrative and, in essence, no longer exist. Have we really ever witnessed this happy end point we're all striving towards?

One might say a happy ending consists of two vital components. One, the feeling of happiness, which I most definitely have. In fact, it's a vital piece of my personal vibration. And two, an ending. And, I mean, here we are, at the end. So consider that box ticked, too. I guess I have, in actuality, delivered a happy ending.

But, ya know, I'm human. And even though I, too, have written myself a new love story, and done the work that I've suggested you do, I admittedly did still hold out hope that Jack, a new Prince Charming or a rough-and-tumble Tramp would sweep in at the last moment to deliver what I believed would be the perfect conclusion. An ending that might tie this all up in a sweet little bow.

But really, to have finished this book still single is actually the perfect ending that none of us saw coming (least of all me). Plot twist! Because this book, although a brilliant guide to dating differently, is at its core about getting to know yourself, strengthening your own vibration and fulfilling your own needs. But in order to be happy and single, does this mean you have to be happy to BE single? In the last few throes of the book-writing process, this distinction became crystal clear. Here's how …

You see, I wrote the last third of this book at the start of the 2020 COVID-19 pandemic, and while we were all forced into self-isolation, many of us (read: singles living alone) were far more isolated than others. I was one of them. And while self-isolation does make for wonderful conditions to complete the first draft of your latest book, it also highlights certain pressure points in, well, all facets of your life. The fact that the subject matter of said book was dating, love and relationships, and there I was sitting in my loft studio all on my lonesome, made me realise two vital things:

1. Wow, I am so grateful that the only person I have to think about it in self-isolation is myself.

But also

2. Wow, it would be really nice to be isolating with someone special right now.

As a fiercely independent woman, I had a brief moment where I felt I needed to stand up for my fellow singles and declare 'We're fine! We've got this!' But what I realised as I sat down to my solo gourmet dinner (because, bored) and glass of expensive red wine (because, treat yo'self), is that although we do 'got this', it's also okay to be happy and completely capable on your own and still not want to be.

It took a global health crisis for me to realise this. For me to boldly proclaim that it's okay to want to have company, to crave connection, to have someone to sleep next to, cook dinner with, laugh with and get into petty quarantine arguments with, and not see this desire as a sign of weakness. It's not wrong to want these things from another, but a very important distinction needs to be made. Write this down, and never forget it ...

Wanting to share your life with someone is a beautiful thing and there is absolutely nothing wrong with feeling like you can't live without someone, as long as you know that you can. (Repeat for effect.)

Okay, let's recap what you've learned thus far:

♥ In Part One of this book you took a journey deep into self-awareness, self-development and self-acceptance. You determined your personal values, learned the importance of listening to your intuition, learned how to identify and strengthen your personal vibration and, most importantly, what compromises and weakens it. And all of this before you even started dating. You discovered that a whole person doesn't need someone else to complete them, and that if you do find yourself with a gaping hole in your life, the most beneficial thing you can do is to ask yourself, *How can I fill this hole myself?*

♥ In Part Two you learned that the essence of love is a lot simpler than we have made it out to be. Over time, we have complicated it with our own stories, which are influenced by what we experienced growing up, what we've seen in movies or read in our favourite romance novels, and what we've experienced in all of our past relationships. So you stripped your story back and rewrote it, thereby creating an incredibly magnetic love vibration to take out for a test run on the dating scene.

♥ In Part Three we discovered that dating is nothing to be feared, especially when you enter with a strong personal vibration. You picked up some foolproof ways to land a hot date, some sweet moves to try on the first and second dates, and also learned how to exit an exchange without disappearing like the great Houdini. Hopefully, you'll be less likely to avoid heartbreak now you know that it won't actually break you, and more likely to notice if you're playing out the same old dating scenarios – and look at the energetics behind these patterns if you are.

And now we're here at the end of the book, but not the end of your story or mine. I hope this book has guided you towards a stronger personal vibration. I hope it's highlighted for you all of the things in your life that make you feel whole, bring you joy and ignite the pure essence of love inside of you. I hope it's inspired you to be unashamedly yourself in all of life's experiences, knowing that when you are vibrating at your highest frequency, you're attracting that which is in full alignment with you into your orbit. And yeah, the plus side of all of this work is that you'll likely (read: definitely) attract rewarding dating experiences into your life, and if all goes to plan, then those dates will likely progress into a higher love.

But if it doesn't happen straight away, and a bunch of toads still cross your path, promise me you won't give up. There might be some room for improvement, but it's helpful to also factor in your lifestyle, universal timing, and walking around with your heart closed, your walls up and your eyes glued shut. I'm guilty of the last three, for sure. BUT also know that it's okay to be single because you simply haven't found the person that you want to share your life with yet.

And this is really where the final part of the Manifestation Equation – the faith piece – falls into place. The pursuit of a higher love, the kind of love that lifts you up, connects you more deeply than ever before with yourself, and allows you to experience a love that gives you strength and makes you feel brave, requires a deep sense faith. Faith not just in yourself and your worthiness of acquiring the kind of love you long to create with another but also that you're being fully supported by a force much greater than you. I call this the universe, but you can call it whatever you damn well like.

Fly your own flag

As I was sitting in isolation writing the final chapter of this book, three texts came through to my phone in the space of an hour.

Text 1

> *Hey hon, hope the book writing's going well. Guess what? I'm pregnant.*

Text 2

> *Jord! How's the book going? Almost done? Will you be finished in time to attend my wedding?*

Followed by a picture of stunning manicured fingers and a gigantic engagement ring.

Text 3

> *Introducing our beautiful bundle of joy,*. Arrived early yesterday morning. Mum, Bub and Papa are doing fine. P.S. How's the book?*

Followed by an adorable pic of a brand-new family of three.

* *Insert cute and slightly quirky baby name.*

It's quite the emotional roller-coaster when you feel genuinely elated for your friends, whose lives are seemingly progressing in the direction you expected or, at the very least, hoped yours would, but at the same time like you've somehow been left behind.

I share this not for sympathy, but for a balance to the comparison that perhaps you too are guilty of when the years pass by, the clock ticks and you're the single friend you vowed you'd never become. And this is why developing your personal vibration is such an asset. To remind you of your strengths in the times when you feel defeated and weak.

I am confident enough in who I am and the frequency of my personal vibration to see why I am still single. Psst: I am about to stand up for myself and fly my own flag. Ego tells me *Don't*. Modesty tells me *Shhh*. But honesty and heart say *No, they need to hear it!* So here goes ...

I could have married and had babies with (realistically) four men. One was nice but boring. One was devoted to me but borderline unstable. One was funny, kind and smart, but I didn't love him, and I couldn't force it. One was safe, but none of our values were aligned. People have told me I'm picky. They're right, I am. But I'm confident in saying that I'm not just looking for company, some offspring and a certain level of security. I'm looking for a higher love, and until I find it, I'm okay with being seated at the singles' table.

I've spent far too long creating a higher love for myself to compromise it for someone who pulls me out of that strong vibration. A weakened personal vibration is of no use to them or me. So please, start by finding a deep, intimate and unwavering higher love for yourself, and I promise the rest will fall into place.

As you turn the final pages of this book, know that you can be a high-vibrating independent person AND still want to be in a relationship. It doesn't make you less whole, it makes you human, and humans crave connection. So, if your happy ending is that you have realised you are a whole person who stands proudly in their authenticity and is ready to attract an equally whole and authentic person to rise in love with, then my work is done. Because a person with a high personal vibration doesn't actually require someone else to give them their happy ending. What they desire is a person who will complement their continually evolving existence so that they can create a higher love, together.

Go forth, sprinkling love vibrations like confetti. Immerse yourself in the celebration of a higher love – first for yourself and then for others, and for your whole wonderful life.

With thanks

Writing a book about love is no easy feat! This book was a bitch to birth, I'm not going to lie. And if it wasn't for an exceptional support team, I'm not sure I would have finished it.

Hollie, I couldn't have written this book without you. Honestly. Not only did you lovingly read every chapter as I wrote it with just enough enthusiasm to encourage me to keep going, but you also wiped away countless tears, listened as I lived through each experience in the book over and over again and gave me permission to experience the full spectrum of emotions. I cannot imagine doing life without you.

Mum! You spent hours on the phone to me as I read each chapter aloud. I honestly don't know anyone else who would do that? You are my guardian angel and I love you so much!

Ruby! Nobody listens to my dating stories with as much interest and curiosity as you. Thank you for being a sounding board and an endless source of support. Your love and friendship mean the world to me. And thank you for Leo – she has been the highlight of every week from the moment she was born. You did good!

To my Byron support crew, Katie, Caitlin, Erin and Noah. The walks, the feeds, the wines and the deep heartfelt chats about boys, heartbreak, writing and bingeworthy TV shows honestly got me through this book-writing process. I am so grateful to have found a team of people to call my soul friends. Each one of you goes above and beyond in the friendship stakes and I feel pretty goddamn lucky.

Zoe, my love! It's official I cannot write a book without you. As integral as you were to *Make It Happen*, you really stepped it up a notch with *Higher Love*. Never have I been so tested. Never have I felt so collapsed and then equally so restored. You are pure magic and I love you beyond measure.

To all the boys I've loved before who 'broke' my heart in ways I thought I could never repair, but then miraculously did. Thank you for the experiences that have shaped who I grew to become but that do not define how I choose to give, receive or experience love.

A special shout-out to J-Swift for trusting me with our story and allowing my words the freedom to craft a truthful and heartfelt narrative. You're a stand-up human who touched my heart in ways we never predicted (and just in time for you to be immortalised in book form).

Laura Kelly, thank you for your help with research, diving into the world of relationship experts and listening to countless love songs. That time you were ghosted by the ghosting expert will go down as one of the funniest experiences during this whole writing process.

To my publisher, Kelly Doust, thank you for always being in my corner with book decisions, and respecting my opinions when they differ from everyone else's. I love the relationship we've cultivated over these two books, and hope it continues long into the future.

Katie Bosher, I was so thrilled to be able to work on the second book with you after the fun we had editing the first. Thank you for your patience with my excessive overuse of certain words and for pointing out that phrases like 'filling all your holes' might come across the wrong way. (I actually still laugh every time I think about it.)

Big shout-out to Julie Mazur Tribe, Viv Valk and the rest of the Murdoch crew. I am so chuffed to be part of such an inclusive publishing family. It's been an absolute treat making books with you.

Index

related to love 136, 136–141

Verinder, Erin Lovell 76

Vibration, Law of. *See also* personal
  vibration.
  definition 13
  role of in Manifestation Equation
    12
  role of polarity in 268–269
  also mentioned 16, 22, 47, 52,
    62, 96

victims, people who identify as 67

vulnerability 249, 250, 256, 258,
  282
  communicating with 286
  as effect of desire to be seen
    62–63
  encouraging others to show 219

W

wholeness, feelings of 20–22,
  80–81